RECOVERY OF SOUL

RECOVERY OF SOUL

A HISTORY AND MEMOIR OF THE CLINICAL PASTORAL MOVEMENT

RAYMOND J. LAWRENCE

CPSP press
New York

© 2017 Raymond J. Lawrence

9 8 7 6 5 4 3 2 1

CPSP Press
432 West 47th Street
New York, NY 10036

www.cpsppress.org

Cataloging-in-Publication Data

Lawrence, Raymond J., 1934-

Recovery of soul: a history and memoir of the clinical pastoral movement / Raymond J. Lawrence.

Includes bibliographical references and index | New York, NY: CPSP Press, 2017.

ISBN-13: 978-0692985991 | ISBN-10: 0692985999

1. Clinical pastoral education (Movement)--History--20th century. 2. Pastoral counseling. 3. Pastoral psychology. 4. Psychology of Religion 5. United States--Church history--20th century

LCC BV4012 .L39 2017 | DDC 207/.1/1--dc23

Cover by Lauren Kay-Jin Kuo | Layout by Krista Argiropolis

For

The Rev. Allison Stokes, Ph.D.

and

Robert Charles Powell, M.D., Ph.D.

The two who did the most to preserve the unlaundered memory

of Anton Theophilus Boisen and his work,

and did so against formidable resistance.

We and posterity will remain in their debt.

"The growing congeniality of psychotherapy and religion is one of the most vitally important movements in the church's life in my generation."

~ Harry Emerson Fosdick[1]

ACKNOWLEDGEMENTS

I am much indebted to Perry Miller and David Roth, who provided continuing valuable consultation throughout my work on this monograph.

I want to express my appreciation to Howard Pendley, for broadly proof-reading the text and helping to make it more readable.

Finally, my appreciation to Cynthia Olson, who used her expertise as a professional editor to put the final touches on questions of grammar, spelling, punctuation, and sense.

Any errors that remain are likely due to last minute tampering with the text on my part. Finishing a text is like sending a child to college. There is always one more thing to say. As Brian Childs likes to say, "One never finishes a text; one must simply abandon it." I have been notoriously irresolute in my obligation to abandon this text.

CONTENTS

Acknowledgements vii
Contents x
Foreword xii
Preface xviii
Prologue 1
1. Boisen 3
2. Helen Flanders Dunbar 19
3. The Emergence of Seward Hiltner 27
4. The Legacy of Russell L. Dicks 35
5. The First Quarter Century 42
6. The Tower of Babel Redux 51
7. Wilhelm Reich: The Orgone and Pastoral Clinicians 59
8. Speaking with One Voice: The Creation of the ACPE 64
9. My Own Entry into the Clinical Pastoral World 70
10. Armen Jorjorian and the Murder of John Rollman 75
11. The Emergence of Women 80
12. The George Buck Case 85
13. Joan E. Hemenway 90
14. The ACPE Underground Report 95
15. The Demonization of the White Male 99
16. The Sex Survey 105
17. Cigarettes, Whiskey, Women, and Poker 111
18. Dialogue 88: Debacle in Minneapolis 116

19. The Dictionary of Pastoral Care and Counseling 125
20. The Creation of the College of Pastoral Supervision and Psychotherapy (CPSP) 130
21. The Battle of Breckenridge 136
22. The Genius of Donald Capps 143
23. Myron C. Madden 147
24. Wayne Oates 151
25. Attacking the Sexual Counterrevolution 154
26. Anonymous 157
27. And from the Distaff Side 160
28. A Revelatory Tale 162
29. Now at this Juncture 165
30. A Personal Detour 172
31. Last Words 175
Appendix 185
Letters from Wayne Oates to Raymond Lawrence 185
Endnotes 191
Postscript—Apropo of Freud's Own Sexual Life 203
About the Author 207

FOREWORD

Origin stories are important. Most religions have them. The religions of Abraham certainly have them. The Hebrew Bible contains several accounts of creation including a secondary story depicting a great flood. Floods are common in many stories of origin. Most stories of origin involve some sort of conflict as can be found in some of the ancient Middle Eastern religions. The early Greek polytheistic religions upon which Homer and the early dramatists relied explained how the people got to where they were and why and perhaps what needed to happen to return to the quiet places. Most Eastern cultures and probably every culture have some form of story about beginnings.

In America, we are all familiar with stories about the origin of the nation. Lately there has been a real surge of interest in the national founding story because of the musical *Hamilton*. Of course, we all know the stories of Washington and his crossing of the Delaware or as a youth chopping down a cherry tree. There is also Paul Revere and of course the Tea Party and slogans such as "Don't Tread on Me."

Nonetheless one need not be a hard-core deconstructionist in the mold of Foucault to understand that George Washington and the cherry tree is not about history as objective fact but rather something else. The apocryphal story is an idealized morality piece undergirding an origin myth about the goodness and moral superiority of the nation's founders. Yes, the Broadway hit *Hamilton* also mythologizes one of the founders though with a bit more humanity than the story of the cherry tree about Washington. Hamilton had his feet of clay and Aaron Burr though not a totally likeable fellow, was a staunch abolitionist and argued for a law ensuring universal suffrage for women. He argued for both prior to 1776. Burr's virtues have been kept largely silent in order not to detract from the prevailing myth asserting the power of those who recount it: the stories told by the victors. This kind of history is a supporting and explanative narrative: *geschichte* not *historie*.

Clinical Pastoral Education/Training has its own stories of origin. While the stories of origin may have some commonalities, say, the same founding personalities, emphasis on the character of one or the other forms the narrative and points to what the narrative holds to be significant. One narrative favors Anton Boisen and the other Richard Cabot. The Cabot version is in a sense more structured and hierarchical and understands itself as more progressive than the Boisen narrative. This position argues for a Hegelian progressive maturity and refinement of the movement such that, while it recognizes its beginnings and those personalities involved, it understands the movement as reaching a plateau in 1967 when the Association for Clinical Pastoral Education (ACPE) was founded. ACPE represented an amalgam of clinical training philosophies represented by various organizations. Its apologists see ACPE as the denouement, a force of history coming into its essence. Many others saw the founding as a political kidnapping. At any rate, this narrative provides for its participants a formula or guide for honing skills and right practice as defined by its own standards of practice. Its theology is Wesleyan perfectionism.

The Boisen narrative is less orthodox in that it recognizes creativity as being a result of conflict, recognizes ambivalence, and is highly suspicious of centralized and transcendent authority. This narrative is focused through the lens or perspective of psychodynamic psychology and liberal empirical theology as implied by terms such as conflict, ambivalence, and transcendent authority. The Boisen narrative understands its participants as guided by small peer groups that provide the authority of collegial relationships within a supervisory accountability. Its theology, it could be claimed, is ambivalent: *simul justus et peccator*.

Both narratives coexisted for many years, perhaps unhappily, and both still exist in some form in both ACPE and CPSP. It must be remembered that CPSP was founded by members in good standing (legalistically if not existentially) of ACPE. These clinical pastoral educators/trainers intended to form an interest group of like-minded persons within ACPE as that organization moved away more and more from its theological and psychodynamic roots. Perhaps it was naïve for those supervisors to entertain the idea that they would not be a threat to the dominant narrative of ACPE. ACPE maintained an immune system that did not have any way to accommodate a reform movement. It is ironic that the core group who formed the College of Pastoral Supervision and Psychotherapy (CPSP) remain members of ACPE and recognize ACPE training as certified training. ACPE does not reciprocate its recognition of CPSP training. It does not fit with their narrative. There is no empirical data to disconfirm the equivalence of the respective training. The dissonance is in the competing narratives though a good argument can be made that the therapeutic aspect of training in ACPE is minimized while in CPSP it is central: skill sets versus recovery of soul.

I introduce this work by Raymond Lawrence as an example of the meaning and efficacy of the Boisen CPSP narrative. Even more, it is the signal example. Because of its first-person quality it cannot be duplicated. His story is one that can be told only by one who was there; who was a witness; who was a player; who knew the central characters and is in touch with those who remain.

This contribution to our understanding of the fits and starts of the clinical pastoral movement exemplifies *simul justus et peccator*. His story is one about the recovery of soul. For there to be a recovery there must be a loss. Lawrence pulls no punches. He acknowledges all our brokenness including that of the founders and leaders, while he also points out the redemptive power of love. The power of love is particularly evident as he remembers the profound impact several figures had on him, particularly his legendary supervisor Armen Jorjorian. At the same time, he does not suffer fools lightly. He also acknowledges that he too has worn the foolscap.

This work has integrity. Unlike most narratives of origin this one is intentionally open ended. Its integrity is that it understands the narrative as always a work in progress. That is owing to Lawrence's brilliance as an interpreter of our origins and of our *raison d'etre*. His narrative is one that is full of humanity, humor, and hope. The road from Boisen to the present does not make the present a denouement; rather, it makes it as a culmination of stories, some not often told or even repressed, but never the end. What we cannot know must be left to silence.

One cannot read much of Lawrence without his writing about the vexations, tribulations, and joys of sexuality. Those of us who know Raymond and who have been his friends and interlocutors eventually will hear about his observations and insights about our sexuality. In fact, Lawrence would be in favor of a comment made by professor at Princeton and whose course I audited when I was teaching at the seminary there. Joyce Carol Oates began a seminar on the 19th and 20th Century novel by saying: "There are three things that hold all novels together that being love, death, and sex... oh, and sometimes food."

Most of us are familiar with Lawrence's work on sexuality: The *Poisoning of Eros: Sexual Values in Conflict* as well as *Sexual Liberation: The Scandal of Christendom*. He applies his critical eye to the role of sexuality, repressed sexuality, sexual politics, and even sexual hypocrisy as it is found within the movement. His description and interpretation of sexual and gender politics within ACPE can be sad; people have been terribly hurt and aggrieved by the politics. Careers have been damaged or ruined. People have been intimidated and silenced. But Lawrence also points to the downright silliness in the expression of the ambivalence by many of the characters in his story. His description of one National meeting of ACPE (Dialogue 88) that bubbled over with sexual politics is one of great pathos: both comedy and tragedy.

Now, in line with Lawrence's acknowledgment of our fallibility, I do have some reservations with some of his understanding of the narrative. These are reservations and certainly not dismissive or negatively critical. Lawrence asked me to write this as a critical introduction. That is what he expects of me. So, I do have some reservations, perhaps not essential ones, but reservations nonetheless.

For instance, with a bit of hyperbole, Lawrence claims that Freud "saved" Boisen's life. I do not know about that. If anyone "saved" Boisen's life one could make a better case for William Bryan, the psychiatrist superintendent of Worcester State Mental Hospital who hired Boisen and where he convened the first clinical training program now known as CPE. Perhaps one could also make a case that a member of that first CPE group, Helen Flanders Dunbar, had a salvific influence on his life. I would also like to nominate Harry Stack Sullivan for that honor as well.

I understand that Lawrence's comment about "lifesaving" is not to be taken literally. I think what he is saying is that psychoanalysis and psychodynamic psychology allowed for Boisen a way to exercise his genius in his own self-understanding and in understanding extreme emotional illness in others. That psychodynamic psychology gave him the medium to develop a profound method of theological and clinical education is undeniable. I am not so sure that Boisen was a Freudian. He certainly found Freud's description and understanding of transference as powerful. This is especially true for Boisen's coming to grips with his own illness and his expression of the "Family of Four" as he explains it in his autobiography *Out of the Depths*. However, in addition, in that autobiography Boisen takes psychiatrists English and Pearson to task for being too uncritical of Freudian psychology in their textbook *Common Neuroses of Children and Adults*. Boisen seems quite open to other psychologists as well, such a Jung and his notion of the "racial unconscious" and the work of Adolf Meyer and his notion of biopsychosocial locus of health and illness. I think that there is a good deal of work to be done, too, in understanding the impact of Sullivan on Boisen. Yes, Boisen read Freud and understood Freud but no, Boisen was not a Freudian.

I wish that Lawrence had included in this work some insight about the internal workings of CPSP over its 27 years. Of course he does have a chapter about the beginnings of CPSP and its vocal anlage in *Contra Mundum* and *The Underground Report*, but he does not have much to say about the workings of this organization. In many ways CPSP's recognition of our brokenness as we try, as Boisen would say, to put a lid on chaos, is fertile ground for a good deal of internal strife and conflict. Lawrence does not have much to say about this essential part of the CPSP narrative. I held a public office in CPSP during a most turbulent and frankly dangerous time when I was president elect in 2013 and president from 2014 to 2016. There was an outright rebellion during those years by a very vocal and destructive minority. Some split off from CPSP and formed their own group. Sound familiar? Perhaps this current work is not the place for Lawrence to focus his keen and insightful eye on the topic of CPSP and its attraction to flux, if not chaos. Perhaps that work will be in the future for us to anticipate. This current work is more global as it looks at the bigger picture from Boisen to now. We can hope that he will attempt a narrowly focused look at CPSP in future work. I hope so.

My reservations are clearly minor. My admiration for this marvelous work is considerable. I think the reader will agree. To borrow from Mark 13 (the little apocalypse): "Let the reader understand. Those who have gone before were on the ride of their lives. You are called to ride along. What a ride it is and ever shall be."

Brian H. Childs, Ph.D.
Diplomate Supervisor and Diplomate Psychotherapist (CPSP)
Community Professor of Bioethics
Mercer University School of Medicine
Savannah, Georgia

PREFACE

This monograph attends to the past, not the future. But how we remember and interpret the past will likely determine how we shape the future. My hope is that this account will be edifying for those who will shape the future of the clinical pastoral movement. One could say that this is my blessing on them, my hope of preparing them for some of the vital issues they will be required to engage for the good of the wider clinical pastoral movement, and indeed the whole human community.

This work is a hybrid, a mixture of history and memoir. Colleagues have argued that it should be two separate accounts. Perhaps. But for me it has been one story. From the beginning of the Boisen movement until 1967, I had no personal connection with it, had not heard of Boisen, and was only slightly cognizant of the clinical pastoral movement that he inaugurated. For the most part I learned the history of the movement by being immersed in it. Otherwise I relied on written material, letters, documents and above all, the oral tradition. I discovered that Boisen's movement had profoundly shaped my life's work, though I was not aware of this until I got involved in it. From 1967 onward I became significantly involved—immersed—in clinical pastoral work and the larger movement as well. It became my principal vocation. Thus the second half of this book, more or less, is based largely on my own personal experiences subsequent to 1967, the year I undertook my first clinical training, and coincidentally the year of the founding of the Association for Clinical Pastoral Education (ACPE). There is certainly an abundance of material in the various archives, particularly those of the Association for Clinical Pastoral Education (ACPE), to which I did not seek access, and which may cast further light on the story and may even challenge and correct some of my claims. Without doubt, others will have experienced the events of the movement differently from the way I have described them. No one has 20/20 vision in all directions at once. Even strong writing and strong opinions should be marked by a certain humility. As Karl Barth was prone to say, referring to his own views, "It could be that things are totally different from what they seem to be."[2] Speaking for myself, I have given here a truthful and accurate account from my own perspective. To the reader I say I hope this account is pleasant reading, edifying, and truthful. Or at least very close to truth.

I owe a great debt to Edward Thornton, who in 1970 published the first, most detailed and highly reliable history of the clinical pastoral movement. Of course, he included nothing subsequent to 1970. Thornton was born of Baptist missionary parents in Iloilo, in the Philippines, at the seminary of Central Philippine University where I actually was a visiting professor in 2015. It was haunting to be aware that the earlier faculty had been killed by the invading Japanese army when I was a child. Thornton ultimately became professor of Pastoral Care at Southern Baptist Seminary in Louisville. Had I had a professional relationship with Thornton in his active years, I likely would have been something of an adversary. He was committed mostly to the Cabot tradition in the clinical pastoral movement and to the Institute for Pastoral Care, and was somewhat wary of their ideological adversaries, Boisen, Freud, and the Council for Clinical Training of Theolical Students tradition. However, a close reading of Thornton's history reveals him to be an eminently fair and careful historian. I consider him to be exceedingly reliable. Though committed more to the Cabot tradition than that of Boisen, I found Thornton to be consistently even-handed—even generous—in his historical judgments.

I never met Thornton in person and had only one conversation with him, by telephone, on March 27, 2002. I called to see if he might speak to the annual College of Pastoral Supervision and Psychotherapy (CPSP) Plenary Meeting. As I introduced myself, not knowing whether in his retirement he had heard of CPSP, he was very responsive, congenial, and affirming. "Yes, I've heard about you rebels!" he said, with some excitement in his voice. "I am glad you're doing what you're doing. From tidbits I hear that you have fire in your belly. Congratulations on creating CPSP. ACPE has become just another organization, with rules and so forth." He said he could not speak at the Plenary meeting because he was not traveling anymore. He had some kind of mild cranial impairment that was progressive. Otherwise he related that he was in very good spirits and among good friends like Clarence Barton, whom, incidentally, I knew and liked, and with whom I myself had worked on ACPE certification committees. He also mentioned that he was a friend of my dear friend Myron Madden. He did add that he felt that his own book on the history of the clinical pastoral movement had not been given its due attention in the movement at large. That is congruent with my memory as well. His book was published the year of my own certification by the ACPE, 1970, yet I never heard anyone speak of the book during my early years of supervising. If he had not produced the book, a great deal of important material would likely have been lost to history, or at best, buried in various archives.

Thornton had come into the clinical training movement by way of Wayne Oates and the outliers of the Southern Baptist Association for Clinical Pastoral Education, the most psychoanalytically oriented of all the groups of pastoral clinicians. Thus it is odd that he finally gravitated to Cabot. That may be a question for some future researcher to pursue.

Subsequently, CPSP presented its 2008 Annual Helen Flanders Dunbar Award to Thornton, in absentia, in March of that year. Thornton died the following September 17 at the age of 83. I consider Thornton one of the key leaders of the early clinical pastoral movement. And in my brief communication with him he was exceedingly gracious.

My major primary historical sources, and the ones I consider most reliable in addition to Thornton, are Robert Charles Powell, Allison Stokes, Seward Hiltner and Charles "Chuck" E. Hall.

In one of those puzzling historical convergences, the inaugural year of the newly formed conglomerate, the ACPE, was 1967. That year the disparate subgroups of the Boisen movement united into one and called themselves the ACPE. But 1967 was also the proverbial year of "The Summer of Love," the zenith of the 20th century's Sexual Revolution. The convergence of the zenith of these two social movements in 1967 is both memorable and disconcerting. The two movements were *prima facie* alien one to the other. But were they? Each was a case of the "letting loose of hope," to borrow from the late Donald Capps. We could say that 1967 was for both movements a time of optimism and hope for the future, but also a time of naive blindness to the profoundly disruptive forces lying just below the surface in both movements. In spite of "The Summer of Love," the wider culture was in turmoil. The Vietnam War was heading for a bad end. Assassinations of progressive leaders were epidemic. The relationships between the genders were heading for a serious disruption, and sexuality itself would soon be profoundly tarnished by powerful unconscious and irrational forces, not least of which was the epidemic societal fantasy that children were being sexually abused everywhere. The Sexual Revolution would soon be eclipsed by a powerful sexual counterrevolution. The newly formed ACPE would soon be similarly tarnished by the same lack of attention to powerful and largely unconscious forces in its own life. The conflicting philosophies of Boisen and Cabot were largely repressed and forgotten in 1967, but the differences were not going to be sloughed over or ignored for very long. Both the hopeful optimism of the Summer of Love and of the happy unity of pastoral clinicians in 1967 were destined to give way to darker, more negative impulses, of which many are yet to be exorcised and thrive among us still.

I hope what I have written in this monograph casts some light on this complex, accursed, and redemptive story.

PROLOGUE

Wayne Oates was arguably among the most influential of American clerics in the 20th century. He was a Southern Baptist minister, or in common parlance, "a preacher." He was born into the mill-town poverty of Greenville, South Carolina, in 1917. In one of his earliest experiences as a young minister, in 1944, he received a call from a woman who had been told directly by her physician that she should "call the preacher." Oates arrived at the woman's home to find her confined to her bed and unable even to care for her personal needs. Oates listened at length to her story of marital unhappiness, personal guilt, and morbid despair. As a novice minister Oates felt unprepared to help her in any way. Nevertheless he sat and listened patiently to her bleak account, her tale of woe. Oates left her with the feeling that he was grossly inadequate to deal with such intractable human suffering.

Shortly thereafter he discovered, to his amazement, that the woman who had been unable to get out of bed was now socializing in her neighborhood. He found out that after he had left her, she rose from her bed, cleaned the house, and returned to the routine of her life. Then he received a call from the referring physician, with a bit of advice. "We are entering upon a whole new understanding of the nature of disease," the physician said to him. "I believe this will draw the minister closer to the work of a doctor. You train yourself for this. I don't know where you will get the training, but wherever you can find anybody who knows anything about it, listen to him."[1]

Oates followed the physician's counsel. He began working part-time with Ralph Bonacker, a clinical pastoral supervisor with the Council for Clinical Training, and a protégé of Anton Boisen. Bonacker was chaplain at the nearby Norton Infirmary, in Louisville, and teaching pastoral care and counseling at Southern Baptist Theological Seminary. The following summer Oates joined Richard K. Young and others for a training unit under Anton Boisen himself at Elgin State Hospital in Chicago.

Oates then went on to do his Ph.D. He wrote his thesis on Sigmund Freud. It could be said that he had discovered on his own a large part of what Freud himself learned on his own, and even before he knew anything about Freud, that attentive listening is the large part of the therapeutic task, and sometimes is even the whole of the therapeutic task. Next he had to learn from Boisen and others what Freud calls "making connections"—connections to past history and connections to the unconscious. Finally, Oates had grasped the pastoral counseling task. He had learned the wisdom of Freud's immortal line, "All I do is listen and make connections." And of course Freud might have added, "Sometimes all I do is listen." It's a simple injunction. And so few have grasped it.[2]

1.
BOISEN

"... so long as the church is in existence and so long as it retains any influence whatsoever, the minister will be engaged in the same general task as the psychiatrist. Regardless of the name we use, for better or for worse, he will be doing psychotherapeutic work."
—Anton T. Boisen[1]

Anton Theophilus Boisen was born in 1876 in Bloomington, Indiana, the home of Indiana University where his father and grandfather were professors. At the same time, a-not-very-distant crow flight away, in Battle Creek, Michigan, John Harvey Kellogg, M.D., was working on foods that would reduce sexual desire in his total war on masturbation. When Boisen reached the age of two, Kellogg invented Corn Flakes. Soon to follow was Granola. C. W. Post then invented Post Toasties and the Rev. Sylvester Graham inspired the invention of Graham Crackers. All these foods were designed to lower sexual desire and therefore reduce the impulse to masturbate, presumably in boys and men. That was the theory, but one that never seems to have been scientifically authenticated. Dr. Kellogg recommended for boys an even more extreme method than diet. He proposed surgical sutures, tying the penis to the testicles in a way that would prevent an erection, or at least to make an erection quite painful. Kellogg and his kind were not mere oddballs in the social order. They had a significant public following. Kellogg, incidentally, was concerned about more than masturbation. He lived with his wife, caring for many orphan children—a very noble commitment—but never during their entire marriage did Kellogg and his wife engage in sexual relations.[2]

This phobic attention to masturbation was not isolated to the American Midwest. It was widespread. The notion blossomed in Europe in the same decade, and according to Elizabeth Roudinesco in her *Freud in His Time and Ours,* was earlier promoted by Jean-Jacques Rousseau in 1762.[3] In both Europe and America, hunts were on for evidence of masturbation, and strong efforts were made to counter it.

Into that heightened hysterical context Boisen was born. His parents were educated and mostly liberal minded. His father was professor of modern languages, and his mother was the first woman student at Indiana University. But when his mother found little Anton playing with his genitals at age four, she, with her husband, rushed little Anton off to the family physician, who circumcised him on the spot. Though it is impossible to prove cause and effect, it seems that this event profoundly shaped Boisen's entire life. And he must have thought it did, because he highlighted the episode in his autobiography published five years before his death. It also seems that Boisen never fully recovered from this war on sex going on all around him in his very early years. He seems to have introjected this parental and cultural view of sexual pleasure. Thus, some 30 years later when he was incarcerated at Westboro State Hospital due to a psychotic break, he twice attempted to castrate himself. As he puts in his own words, he was "only partially successful." This may mean that he excised, by his own hands, only one testicle. A physician sutured his scrotum. Boisen seems to have attempted to complete what his mother started. This self-castration was apparently included in earlier versions of his autobiography, but excised on demands of his family, specifically his sister. It is not known what other embarrassing details were excised from Boisen's original text. Chaplain Sullivan of Elgin State Hospital, where Boisen died, told Henri Nouwen that so much was excised from Boisen's original text that the publisher nearly refused publication.[4]

In 1905, at a point of confusion, the 29-year-old Boisen followed a popular pious practice alleged to provide a relevant word from God to deal with an immediate problem. He blindly opened his Bible at random and read the line, "Behold thy mother." It was as if Boisen's pathology was conspiring to intensify his craziness. In any case, that simply bonded him more pathologically to his mother.

Boisen's father had his own problems, the details of which are sketchy. He apparently abandoned the family for a brief period, had an affair, and abruptly resigned his teaching position at one point in Anton's young life. At the age of 38, when Anton was seven, he died suddenly of a coronary. A year later Anton discovered neighborhood boys stealing fruit from their pear tree. Anton confronted them and they pointed a nail gun in his face. Anton had heard his grandfather say that blinking was a defensive move, so he resolved not to be defensive, and was determined not to blink when the gun was pointed at his face. The gun was fired. The nail penetrated his pupil, not even injuring the lid. The rest of his life he made do with one eye.

A 20th-century Oedipus, but only half-blinded, Boisen remained a mother's boy all his life. She pampered him and thwarted his growing up and forced him to wear clothes that befitted younger children, which alienated him from his peers to a certain extent. And Boisen remained immaturely attached to his mother into his adulthood, confiding in her even as an adult about troubles he was having with women. When his mother died in 1930, Boisen, who was then 44, had his second major psychotic break. It seems, from a psychoanalytic perspective, that Boisen was neurotically attached to his mother for life and fully absorbed his mother's negativity toward sexual pleasure. He never seems to have had, nor seriously to have sought, treatment for this affliction. He was hospitalized three times, briefly except for the first time, and reveals in his writings that he had two additional brief psychotic episodes.

Nevertheless, Boisen was intellectually very bright. He was even bright enough to be aware that he had serious personal problems largely centered on his sexuality. He enrolled in college and majored in French. But French novels unnerved him with their blatant sexuality. One day for his class he was reading Tolstoy's quasi-French Russian novel, *Anna Karenina,* the story of an adulterous woman. To get a break from the sexual intensity of the story he went outside to burn caterpillars from the trees in his yard, using a long pole with a kerosene-soaked rag tied at the end and lighted. After returning to the novel he heard a commotion, with fire engines, and discovered that he had left the burning pole in the shed while it was still smoldering. He had burned down the shed. Boisen was savvy enough to know that this "accident" was meaningful. As a result he abandoned French altogether and began majoring in forestry. The sexuality of trees would not disturb his psyche.

After his undergraduate studies followed by forestry work, Boisen decided that he had a call to the ministry. He enrolled in Union Theological Seminary in New York in 1908. In his study of Greek he noticed that New Testament words pertaining to sexual sins would fly off the page and hit him in the eye. Again, he was aware enough to know that this was happening only to him and that the experience related to some kind of psychological problem. He even went so far in assertiveness as to persuade the seminary administration to institute its first ever psychology course. However, he was disappointed with the decision to make it a course in the psychology of religion. He wanted a course on psychopathology. He was fully aware that he himself was psychologically disturbed. He simply did not know what to do about it. During his time in seminary he never heard mention of the name of Sigmund Freud, even though Freud was making his only visit to the U.S. during the period when Boisen was a seminarian. He graduated from Union in 1911. Boisen's theological stance, according to Seward Hiltner in a post-mortem assessment, was that of a Harnack-Schweitzer type of liberal. Hiltner added that Boisen also possessed a cautious but deeply felt mysticism, with elements of

American moralism (that was inflexible toward himself but tolerant about others) and the dynamic insights of Freud.[5]

Boisen met the love of his life, Alice Batchelder, in 1902. She was a YWCA worker he courted for the next three decades until her death, and the high probability is that she never permitted him even so much as a kiss on the cheek. Alice was a veritable virago. Most of the time she refused to see him, even when he had traveled some distance in hopes of seeing her. She wrote him countless "Dear John" letters telling him never to contact her again. At other times she led him on. And he persisted, even in some periods of his life in keeping a daily diary, which he forwarded to Alice. If nothing else, he was persistent.

Alice's pattern of relating to Boisen was a vivid illustration of what used to be called schizophrenigenic, that is to say, crazy-making. Alice endlessly repeated the pattern of saying yes today and no tomorrow. But what was even more remarkable was Boisen's acquiescence to her pattern of relating. He wrote her endless numbers of detailed letters, sometimes on a daily basis, rarely getting any kind of response. He was committed to Alice for life, whether she liked it or not. It seems that Boisen had found a perfect replica of his mother, a pattern of behavior not unusual in males.

After seminary Boisen sought pastoral positions and finally found one in the Midwest. Alice lured him into thinking she would go with him, only to tell him at the last minute that she had never had any intention of being a pastor's wife, and certainly not *his* wife. As it turned out, he was not a very successful parish pastor. But during World War I he enlisted with the YMCA and served in France. Returning home after the Armistice he was living with his family and suffered a psychotic episode in the fall of 1920. The family was frightened and called for help. A physician and six policemen took the befuddled Boisen off to Boston Psychopathic Hospital. He was later transferred to Westboro State Hospital for a total forced hospitalization of 15 months.

After a brief period of suicidal attempts and destructively violent protests, Boisen settled down for a compliant hospitalization. A few weeks into his hospitalization his close friend and fellow pastor, Fred Eastman, brought Boisen a copy of Freud's *Introductory Lectures*. The reading of this book seemingly changed Boisen's life. He finally found an authority who understood what Boisen himself was experiencing. He requested that the hospital find a way to get him Freudian psychoanalytic treatment. The closest hospital offering such treatment was Payne Whitney Psychiatric Clinic (now New York Presbyterian Hospital) in White Plains, New York. Westboro agreed to a transfer and a date was set. But the day before the scheduled transfer, Boisen had a relapse. It must be surmised that Boisen both wanted psychoanalytic treatment and was afraid of it, and hence relapsed. We can guess that he would have suspected that treatment would have exposed his pathological relationship with both his mother and Alice. As far as anyone knows, Boisen never had any psychoanalytic treatment subsequently. (Of course, neither did Freud have any psychoanalytic treatment! It seems that the only real treatment for either man was what he gave himself.) Pruyser astutely opined that Boisen always feared that somehow the stringency of superego demands would be "reduced" in analysis, which he saw as a dangerous tinkering with ethics.[6] However, Boisen was released from Westboro with the help of his mother in early 1922.

During his hospitalization at Westboro, Boisen became aware of the great disparity between what Freud wrote about and the kind of treatment he himself was receiving. Freud clearly made it the therapist's task to listen to patients, and in fact to keep on listening until some clarity revealed itself. In Boisen's hospitalization experience no physician would listen to him. He would be allowed 15 minutes of the physician's time, and the physician would do most of the talking. What they generally tried to tell Boisen was that his sexual restraints were too severe, that he needed to loosen up and cease being so rigid about his sexual behavior. Boisen regarded this bit of directive counsel with contempt, and rightly so. Boisen's sexual rigidity was likely related to his bond with his mother, and he was not prepared to sever his maternal connection or to violate her implied injunctions.

Boisen famously said, "The cure has lain in the carrying through of the delusion itself."[7] He felt that his psychotic episodes, as he struggled to understand them, actually made him a better, more integrated person. Unquestionably he became an astonishingly creative person and a shaper of history. But he never got so far as to shake his mother's curse on his sexual life. And in spite of his appreciation of Freud and the psychoanalytic approach, he remained wary all his life that the stringency of the superego demands would be reduced, and that sexual ethics might be diluted. It could be said of Boisen, too, that he saved others but himself he could not save. Boisen was released from psychiatric lock-up by "a charming young doctor" whom he liked very much. But the doctor "disappointed" Boisen when he gave as his final recommendation that Boisen give freer rein to his sexual impulses. That exchange epitomizes Boisen's lifelong struggle, one that in spite of all he accomplished, he never came to terms with.

During his long involuntary hospitalization Boisen found his calling. On his release from psychiatric lockup, and inspired by Freud, Boisen went immediately to Harvard in an attempt to learn the clinical method of treating patients from a well-known physician, ethicist, and founder of medical social work, Richard Cabot. Boisen's vision was to learn the clinical approach and to train ministers clinically, so as to provide them with competence to treat emotionally disturbed persons like himself. Cabot enthusiastically took Boisen under wing and even supported him financially toward fulfilling his dream. Barely two years out of psychiatric confinement, Boisen, with Cabot's help, landed a position as chaplain at Worcester State Hospital. The administrator, William Bryan, was happy to have him. In the face of public criticism—hiring a chaplain to serve crazy people?—Bryan responded that he would hire a horse doctor if he thought it would help his patients. Only much later did it become a consistent national policy to have a chaplain available to work with psychiatric patients.

Boisen hit the ground running at Worcester, starting in July 1924. He was hardly unpacked before he planned for his first clinical pastoral training group, for the summer of 1925. It consisted of four trainees, three male seminarians and Helen Flanders Dunbar, a psychiatrist and a seminarian herself, who became more of a course assistant than a trainee. The summer was not a roaring success. One trainee left after the first day. Another was locked in a closet by a patient, and left once he was rescued. But the program was repeated, greatly expanded over the next five years, and attracted considerable attention in the wider theological community. Dunbar worked with Boisen throughout most of that time. In these very early years the trainees did not even assume the role of chaplains. They did not function as religious authorities at all. Their goal was to understand emotional disturbance and the working of the mind. They worked as salaried orderlies for 10 hours during the day, and at night they reviewed patients' cases. Later they moved to half-time orderly positions. And then still later they abandoned the orderly role altogether, serving as stipended chaplain interns. This method of training caught on and in about a decade became a universal requirement for mainline Protestant seminarians.

Boisen's program at Worcester was not the first that attempted to integrate religion and psychiatry in ministering to patients. The Rev. Dr. Elwood Worcester at Emmanuel Episcopal Church had initiated a program with similar objectives in Boston in 1908. Worcester and two psychiatrists offered a free counseling program to the public, and on the first day 198 persons showed up. The program is often referred to as the first clinical pastoral training program and received wide publicity in magazines such as *Ladies Home Journal*. But it was not psychoanalytically oriented. In 1923 William S. Keller inaugurated a similar program for seminarians at Bexley Hall in Ohio. Seminarians were tutored by social workers. Again, this was not psychoanalytically oriented. These precursors to Boisen were lacking the central critical element of Boisen's mission.

Boisen's programs were quickly gathering a wide and positive reputation, and in 1930 his little coterie incorporated as the "Council for Clinical Training of Theological Students (CCTTS)." Cabot was made president and treasurer, Boisen secretary, Philip Guiles field secretary, and Dunbar Medical Director.[8] Later the same year Boisen's mother died and Boisen had another, albeit brief psychotic break. He visited Cabot and began talking about himself in the third person. Cabot reacted badly, attempted to dismiss Boisen from his own movement, and ended his personal and financial support. This conflict put the handful of newly minted pastoral clinicians with barely a six-year track record immediately into two camps that were not very cordial—the Boisen and Cabot camps. Guiles allied himself with Cabot, and Dunbar allied herself with Boisen. During the subsequent decade Dunbar managed the CCTTS. She gathered around her those who were inspired by Boisen, most notably Seward Hiltner and Carroll Wise, and kept Cabot and his followers at bay. Boisen himself, who never seemed interested in formal organizations, appeared to float above the internecine strife as if it were irrelevant.

In 1932 Boisen moved to Chicago where he took the position of chaplain at Elgin State Hospital and did some teaching at Chicago Theological Seminary. The reason for the move was certainly his wish to be near Alice, but a contributing factor must certainly have been Cabot's judgment that Boisen was a sick man psychologically and not to be trusted. In Chicago Alice and Anton had regular dinner dates, often taking in a concert or some other cultural activity. Alice developed cancer in 1935 and died that fall. Typical of her, at the time of her diagnosis Alice completely severed her relationship with Boisen and did not see him at all as she declined toward her death. Boisen reacted to this final rejection with his last documented psychiatric break. His colleagues rushed him off to Baltimore where he was briefly hospitalized at Shepherd-Pratt Hospital in the weeks before Alice actually died.

It seems that after 1932 Boisen had minimal connection with the leaders of the movement he had founded. In fact, Boisen clearly abandoned the organizational leadership of the clinical pastoral training community he founded. On the face of it, this is puzzling. Certainly he could have exercised his leadership from Chicago, putting Cabot in his rearview mirror. However, Wayne Oates apparently had the key to the riddle. He wrote me shortly before his own death in 1999 that Boisen had told him that he objected to the Council's certification procedures in which some persons were denied certification. Boisen, according to Oates, wanted a community that was open to any interested person. Of course, that would render meaningless the whole notion of certification. However, we note that Richard Cabot, President of the Council in its first year of existence, had declared Boisen himself unworthy of certification. Thus we can assume that Boisen identified with others who might be similarly judged. If the Council could deny Boisen certification, anyone could be a target of such rejection—or in Boisen's case, such degradation. Had Boisen lived through many subsequent decades he surely would have been dismayed by the great numbers of persons who were ruled incompetent to conduct clinical pastoral training programs.

After arriving in Chicago, Boisen created his own "Chicago Council for Clinical Pastoral Training." It reflected his own philosophy of local autonomy. It was apparently short-lived. Boisen seems mostly to have faded from the larger clinical pastoral training landscape by the mid-1940s, though he apparently made cameo appearances at various meetings. He did continue to cultivate his own little clinical pastoral training garden at Elgin State Hospital in Chicago. In 1944 he trained young Wayne Oates and Richard Young, who were destined to exercise key leadership in the movement later. In the late 1940s Boisen did request a financial grant from the Council that he had founded. He asked for $3000 to support a research project, but was denied. That would be approximately $35,000 in today's coinage. At one point the Council even refused to accredit Boisen's own training program at Elgin.

Though Boisen was on the far-out fringe of the organizational aspects of the movement, he did do some significant writing. In 1936 he published *Exploration of the Inner World: A Study of Mental Disorder and Religious Experience*. It was a monumental work. He disclosed his own experience of mental disturbance as well as his disappointment at the shallow and uninformed medical treatment he had received during his psychiatric incarceration. He wrote of the lack of effective treatment he received during his long hospitalization at Westboro.

In the book, Boisen made a strong endorsement of the psychoanalytic treatment of Freud. He declared, echoing Freud, that psychiatric disturbance was an attempt by the mind to solve a problem. In fact, Boisen believed that the problems of sex figured prominently in much mental disturbance. He was also convinced that behavior modification would have had no benefit for him, meaning that he was wiser than most hospital psychiatrists nationally. Boisen proposed in the book that many religious leaders through history emerged out of psychiatric disturbance. He cited George Fox, John Bunyan, Emmanuel Swedenborg, Saul of Tarsus, and others. And Boisen inveighed against the neglect of psychiatric patients by the religious community. He pointed out that while general hospitals typically employed chaplains, there were hardly any chaplains employed at the nation's psychiatric hospitals.

Most significantly, Boisen proclaimed the importance of a psychoanalytic approach to mental disturbance, even if he had not benefited from it personally. And more astutely, Boisen was aware of the subtle differences between Freud and Jung, characterizing Jung as less interested in unconscious material and more committed to didacticism. Boisen was explicit in his judgment that the Freudian psychological posture held more promise than the Jungian. Given the fact of Boisen's uneasiness about sex and the fact that Freud was identified with sex, however distorted that identification was, Boisen's ongoing appreciation of Freud is quite astonishing.

In the late 1950s Boisen wrote his autobiography, *Out of the Depths,* which was published in 1960. It is a monumental work, and it disclosed the fact that he knew what had made him crazy. The book was on the boundary of being rejected due to the interference of his sister, who attempted to bowdlerize it, removing the embarrassing sexual data. She was successful only in part. She did manage to delete the account of Boisen's two attempts to castrate himself, in which he was partially successful.[9] My sources do not reveal the extent to which the sister may have been successful in deleting other sexual material.

We must conclude that Boisen was damaged very early by the peculiar roles played by each of his parents. His father's intermittent absences, sexual exploits, and early death left him entirely dependent on his mother. His abrupt circumcision at age four, with didactic follow-up, damaged him in such a way that he withdrew from any serious attempt to find sexual satisfaction for the rest of his life. In some profound way he internalized the message from his mother that pleasuring himself sexually was unacceptable. That message was likely reinforced by the sudden, early death of his father who had partaken of some illicit sexual adventures. He appears to have internalized that negative innuendo related to sex. This is confirmed by his selection of the virago, Alice Batchelder, as the primary and lifelong object of his affections, an eminently fitting partner for him. Finally, he seems never to have had a full-fledged sexual relationship during his entire life. Boisen, then, must be seen as a tragic figure who lived an emotionally impoverished life. On the other hand, paradoxically, Boisen brought life and freedom to many, and astonishingly, even sexual freedom. While he never experienced psychotherapy personally, as far as is known, he did know that therapy could be salvific for persons like himself.

Boisen lived an ironic life. Permanently crippled emotionally, in need of psychotherapy that he never received, he designed an approach to the training of Protestant ministers that ensured that they would all have at least a sampling of the cure he himself never had. He did for others what he could not find for himself. The first unit of Boisenite clinical training became traditionally a mélange of personal psychotherapy—though never named as such—and skills training. This was an undisclosed and unspoken secret in the Boisen movement. Young Protestant seminarians from the 1930s and onward, until the movement lost steam later in the century, were for the most part radically changed by their brief 12-week initial clinical training experience. Many of them undertook further, advanced training later. And many of them made use of personal psychotherapy later, having had a fragmentary sampler in their first clinical training unit. Even more significantly, these clinically trained ministers typically went on to offer pastoral counseling to their own congregations, counseling that was psychoanalytically informed. And some of them, with further training, left the pastoral profession and presented themselves publicly as psychotherapists.

Henri Nouwen, a great admirer of Boisen, but who seems not to have fully understood him, may have been the last person to make a record of a substantive conversation with Boisen. He made three pages of notes of his August 1964 visit to Boisen in his Elgin State Hospital quarters. He found Boisen sitting in a wheelchair in his "not very clean little room behind the dining hall." There was hardly space for Nouwen to sit. Noises from the kitchen intruded in their conversation. Chaplain Sullivan, the hospital's chaplain, insisted that he should not visit for too long. Boisen was very friendly and expressed gratitude to the hospital for allowing him to board there. Boisen wanted to talk, and he wanted to talk theology. Nouwen had difficulty inserting his own questions into the conversation. "God is the internalization of the highest values of our social relationships," Boisen proclaimed. Boisen told Nouwen that Freud was the most important help in his recovery process and that he had tried to read as much of Freud's work as possible. He felt himself lucky that he had found Freud's work at the right time. When Nouwen asked him about Cabot, Boisen cited Cabot's book, *Differential Diagnosis,* in which he elaborates the case-method approach, a book for which Boisen expressed appreciation and used as a model for his own work with patients. This was a remarkably honest and gracious assessment of Cabot, given Cabot's profound discrediting of Boisen. Both Boisen and Nouwen wanted to talk further, but the hospital chaplain insisted that the visit should not be long. Chaplain Sullivan, acting as a mother hen, seems to have assumed more authority than required.[10]

Two months later, in October 1964, if the oral tradition is accurate, Boisen wandered into the joint annual meeting of the Council and the Institute in a downtown Chicago hotel. George Buck was there, standing, and in conversation with Council leader Tom Klink. Boisen approached the two and greeted them, and a brief, desultory conversation ensued. As Boisen walked away, Klink remarked, "That's just the way he is."[11] The subliminal message from a key leader in the Council to a novice clinician was that Boisen was no longer relevant. That message is congruent with the role Boisen played since 1932 in the movement he had created. He was left bereft of any significant approbation for the monumental contribution he had made, specifically to the Council and generally to American religion.

Many of the pastoral clinicians who were beneficiaries of Boisen's groundbreaking work had negative feelings toward him personally, as Tom Klink seemed to demonstrate. Seward Hiltner, in a tribute to Boisen at the joint meeting of the Council and the Institute in 1965, just 18 days following Boisen's death, after citing his genius, owned that he could be cantankerous. Some of those who worked with Boisen at Elgin in his last decades, such as Herman Eichorn and Clarence Bruninga, expressed their personal dislike of him, viewing him as inflexible and difficult.[12] And the entire movement that he had spawned treated him like a nonperson. Such attitudes might have been anticipated from the Institute members who were followers of Cabot. But such negative feelings were expressed by the Council membership as well. He should have been honored rather than snubbed at that Chicago meeting in 1964 for spawning a revolution in religious practice.

Paul Pruyser visited Boisen near the end of his life and found him "not without humor and delicacy," but he felt that something had happened to his feelings and their expression. He was like "a well-adjusted, chronic schizophrenic...the language is beautiful and the topics are moving but there is something utterly pathetic about it all."[13] Pruyser was viewing Boisen at the end of his life, isolated and without dignity, and certainly bereft of any of the honor due him.

Boisen may have been boorish at times, but he did not accomplish what he did through boorishness. Seward Hiltner wrote of Boisen, "My wife had been hearing, ever since we met, of this great teacher of mine, with all the stories and folklore that had grown up about him. She would have been prepared, I think, if he had been gruff, or had sat all evening in the corner, or had given a lecture over the dessert. When he left she said spontaneously, 'He's charming,' and he was. He listened to her better that I have been able to do before or since."[14]

And Wayne Oates tells the story of his training time with Boisen in Chicago, when Boisen gave over his own living quarters to Oates and his wife because there were no married trainees' apartments available.[15]

If we can assume that Boisen was disliked by many of his own people, as indeed he was, such negative feelings were not universal. We have the record of one clinical supervisor, an Institute supervisor at that, Richard Lehman, who greatly appreciated Boisen and was on very friendly terms with him. Lehman in 1959 happened to be president of the Association of Mental Health Chaplains. That year Lehman and the AMHC honored Boisen, presenting him with "a polished brass clock" that Boisen was said to cherish the rest of his life. Lehman reported that it was still in the Boisen Room at the Chicago Theological Seminary library half a century later.[16] The clock may have been an unconscious reminder that his time was running out.

Boisen died in October 1965, apparently alone, living as a virtual pauper in an unkempt room with only a screen door off the refectory of Elgin State Hospital, where he had served most of his life as chaplain. His notable protégé and successor in 1932 as chaplain at Worcester State Hospital, Carroll Wise, visited him a week before his death. Wise reported him to be emaciated and almost unrecognizable, attempting to enunciate coherently, but unable to do so.

According to Allison Stokes, Boisen always kept a portrait of Dante in his room, a patron of sorts, undoubtedly introduced to him by Dunbar, a recognized expert on Dante.[17] It was fitting. Dunbar and Boisen, as well as Dante, experienced hell.

Anton Boisen died as an outcast. But the redemptive effect of his life is a story that must never be forgotten. In the 1920s Boisen created an enterprise known as clinical pastoral training that made it less likely that any future Protestant minister or any person who was as wounded as he was would be left to wander alone in his psychopathology. In the mid-1930s a three-month experience of clinical pastoral training was made mandatory for almost all Protestant seminarians who sought a theological degree. This meant in turn that a great many church members received from their pastors the benefits of at least a beginning level of psychotherapeutic care. This was a monumental contribution to the leadership of American Protestantism from the 1930s onward. That other historical forces came to bear later in the century is of course another story.

2.
HELEN FLANDERS DUNBAR

Helen Flanders Dunbar was a phenom, an authentic Renaissance woman, born to a wealthy family in Chicago in 1901. At four feet eleven inches in height, she was nicknamed "Little Dunbar" at Wellesley College. But in medical school she acquired the moniker, "The Pocket Minerva." (Minerva was the Roman goddess of wisdom who emerged from the head of Jupiter fully grown, assertive, bearing arms, and became the patroness of medicine, music, poetry, and wisdom.) Dunbar's early moniker was accurate, but the latter was more evocative.

Dunbar made the most of the wealth into which she was born. She became a physician, a psychiatrist, a theologian, a mathematician, and a literary authority on Dante. Her academic work was done at Columbia University, Yale University, and Union Theological Seminary, at points working on three degrees simultaneously. In order to accomplish this she hired secretaries to do some of the research and typing. She was the acknowledged intellectual leader of her undergraduate class at Columbia and won the outstanding student award at Union. Part of her award was a trip to Europe. There she got a therapeutic consult with the Freudian psychoanalyst, Helene Deutsch, and joined in rounds with Deutsch's husband Felix, also a Freudian psychoanalyst. She then visited Zurich and had a number of visits with Jung at Burgholzli. She and Jung shared Christmas gifts. But there is no suggestion made that Dunbar was analyzed in these visits. On the other hand, analysis can be brief as well as extended. Dunbar then visited Lourdes. It is not known why she did not consult with Freud, with whom she seemed to have more in common than with Jung. Perhaps she did and elected not to talk about it. Dunbar was politically astute. This was the same year Freud published *The Question of Lay Analysis.*

Dunbar became known among psychologists as "The Mother of Holistic Medicine." She founded the American Psychosomatic Society in 1942 and was first editor of its journal. She was an instructor at the New York Psychoanalytic Institute from 1941 to 1949. Dunbar typically introduced herself as H. Flanders Dunbar, or simply Flanders Dunbar. As a woman working mostly in a man's world, it was an obvious strategy to open doors that might otherwise not be open to her. It is easy to imagine consternation resulting from this woman of very small statue walking into some prestigious office where the host was expecting the arrival of a certain Mr. Flanders Dunbar.

Dunbar had met with Boisen in the spring of 1925 at Union Theological Seminary, in the midst of her work for her degree in theology. He was soliciting his first clinical pastoral trainees, and she joined his first group that summer. She was of course much more than a trainee, rather more like a course assistant. She remained with him much of the time for the next five years, both learning the clinical discipline and assisting him with his clinical pastoral training programs at Worcester State Hospital. She remained attached to Boisen until he left for Chicago in 1932. At that point, Boisen's protégé, Carroll Wise, succeeded him at Worcester. The program and others like it expanded rapidly, receiving wide attention and attracting increasing numbers of trainees. Apparently clinical pastoral training was an idea whose time had come.

The appearance of Dunbar in Boisen's life, in 1925, was very significant and highly beneficial to him and to the movement he was inaugurating. He soon became physically attracted to her and reported that she "responded to my advances and addressed me by my middle name, Theophilus." Reports suggest that they were close to marrying. But later in life he declared that they had never had a sexual relationship, probably intending to mean a consummated sexual relationship. Whatever the specifics of their personal relationship, Dunbar was deeply important to him, and certainly sexual overtones infused the relationship. Ultimately Dunbar saved Boisen's movement from oblivion.

Boisen informed Alice Batchelder by letter of the appearance of Dunbar in his life, and this provoked Batchelder to do something she had not done in all their 20-year, one-sided relationship. She began writing him substantive letters and, even more remarkably, affectionate letters. Boisen was now attached to two women whom he loved, neither of whom—perhaps—he had ever touched. So he proposed to clarify and solidify this triangular relationship by staging a three-way quasi marriage rite at the chapel in the Hilton Hotel in Chicago on June 2, 1928. Boisen undoubtedly intended platonic relationships with the two. The two women agreed, but at the last minute Dunbar sensibly took a ship to Europe for a time of study. The rite was cancelled. Boisen rescheduled it for the following year, on Thanksgiving Day, but without Dunbar. Batchelder found it "very meaningful." Dunbar had kept her distance from the Boisen-Batchelder relationship, but in March 1930 she traveled to Chicago to meet Alice. The results of that meeting are unknown.[1]

In the sixth year of this clinical pastoral training venture Boisen, Dunbar, Cabot, and their several principal protégés decided that they should incorporate, giving their project official legal status. Thus, in January 1930, they did just that, under the name of the Council for Clinical Training of Theological Students, CCTTS, known popularly as the "C's and the T's." Later it was abbreviated to CCT and popularly referred to as simply "The Council." Cabot was made President and Dunbar, Medical Director. The office of the newly formed corporation was situated in Cabot's Harvard Square home.

Some months after the incorporation, Boisen's mother died, and he responded with yet another psychotic break. He showed up on Cabot's doorsteps talking about himself in the third person. It was not a prolonged break but it unnerved Cabot, who reacted badly, declaring that Boisen was unfit even to be a minister, much less a trainer of ministers. Cabot moved to oust Boisen from the fledgling organization. He did not count on the personal resources of Dunbar, however.

After Boisen's brief psychotic break in response to his mother's death and Cabot's attempt to dismiss Boisen from the fledgling organization, Dunbar took matters into her own hands. She saw that the genius of this movement was centered in Boisen, not Cabot. She arbitrarily and assertively seized the books of the new corporation from Cabot's home office, took a train to New York City, and established new organizational offices in her spacious apartment at 730 Park Avenue.[2] Dunbar had staged a coup d'état. Cabot's disenchantment with Boisen was the genesis of the rift between the two men and their respective views of life that was never healed, and a rift that continues today to affect everyone who is considered to be a pastoral clinician. Cabot remained president until 1935 when he was replaced by the board without notice. He was officially stripped of his authority in the organization, but functionally Dunbar had stripped him of his authority earlier when she moved the locus of the organization, and its records, to New York. From that point on clinical pastoral training developed two geographic and philosophical centers, New York and Boston, personalized specifically by Boisen and Cabot. The New York group was immersed in psychoanalytic theory and practice. The Boston group was more didactic, rooted in educational theory and generally avoiding psychology altogether, especially Freud. It was a philosophical and emotional dispute that has continued even into the present, almost a century later.

Dunbar understood the profound issues at stake in the conflict between Cabot and Boisen. As a psychiatrist herself, she understood and promoted the value of the psychoanalytic perspective and its integral relationship with religion. In part, the battle was over the question of the role of a pastor, whether pastors were going to be psychoanalytically oriented therapists in their own right or adjuncts to the real therapists, the physicians. This ongoing dispute could by now be called another Hundred Years' War.

Had Boisen not been allied with the boldly assertive and imaginative Dunbar, who supported him organizationally and philosophically, it seems doubtful that he or his vision would have prospered. As it was, with Dunbar, like Minerva carrying his weapons, Boisen changed the face of American Protestantism in the 20th century. With her help he became the principal theoretician of clinical pastoral training. Boisen's vision, with Dunbar's support, dominated the clinical pastoral movement for its first 40 years and beyond.

In 1932, Boisen left Boston for Chicago. He took the position of chaplain at Elgin State Hospital, a position he held for most of the next three decades. He also did some teaching at Chicago Theological Seminary. However, the real reason Boisen went to Chicago was to be near Alice Batchelder. That same year Dunbar married Theodore Wolf.

Among Dunbar's many talents was skill in community organizing. With Boisen's move to Chicago, Dunbar essentially took over leadership of the Council for the subsequent decade. Her title was "Medical Director" but she was functionally the CEO. She hired male executive secretaries to front the organization, but she in fact continued to be the power behind the curtain. She first selected Russell Dicks as executive secretary. However, Dicks was a Cabot partisan and soon backed out, moving fully into the Cabot camp, which became known first as "The Cabot Club." Next, in 1935, she hired Seward Hiltner, a young man who had just finished training with Carroll Wise at Boisen's former hospital, Worcester State. Hiltner made his office in a converted maid's room in Dunbar's New York City apartment, and remained with her for three years. Hiltner's successor, in 1938, was Robert Brinkman, who remained as Council Executive until 1946, when he changed his professional identity to that of a psychoanalyst and went into private practice. His assistant, Fred Kuether, succeeded him.

Clinical pastoral training took a major leap forward at the 1934 biennial meeting of the American Association of Theological Schools (AATS, since renamed simply ATS). Dunbar addressed the meeting. She took it by storm in her advocacy of clinical training for seminarians. Hiltner labeled Dunbar's speech "a Billy Graham experience." The result was a resounding affirmation of clinical training by the seminaries of the AATS. Wrote Hiltner, "Dunbar did many positive things for clinical pastoral training in those early years, but none was so spectacular as her conversion of the professors."[3] Dunbar's evangelism for clinical training in relation to the AATS meant that virtually every mainstream seminary in the country was requiring or beginning to require a summer unit of clinical pastoral training prior to graduation, a requirement that was still in force when I enrolled in seminary in the late 1950s, and generally is followed still today. This was a monumental innovation.

Dunbar herself was ousted from her leadership position in the Council in 1942. We must surmise that there was rebellion against her strong personal authority as a woman as well as her close alliance with psychoanalysis and particularly with Freud. And since her previous husband was the preeminent American Reichian and patron of Wilhelm Reich personally, the conventionally religious surely took some offense at that. We can also assume that there was some discomfort with Dunbar among the more conventionally religious concerning innuendoes of Dunbar's sexual freedom in her personal life.

Dunbar's first husband was Theodore P. Wolf, a German émigré whose German name had been Wolfensberger. Wolf visited Norway in 1938 to study under Wilhelm Reich, and he was notable for having translated Reich's work into English. He also helped Reich immigrate into the U.S., leaving Norway on a passenger ship just before the German invasion, in 1939. Dunbar and Wolf divorced that same year. Reich died in 1957 in Lewisburg Federal Penitentiary, in Pennsylvania, where he was imprisoned, convicted of violating the U.S. Food and Drug laws by the use of his orgone box. In 1940 Dunbar married George Henry Soule, Jr., editor of *The New Republic,* who outlived her.

After she was forced out of her leadership position at the Council by the Administrative Committee in June 1941, Dunbar seems to have had nothing more to do with the clinical pastoral movement. At the time about 20 clinical pastoral training centers were in operation under the auspices of the Council, a number that remained steady during the war years, according to Thornton.[4] The reason for Dunbar's fall from grace is not known to me. Perhaps somewhere in the Council's archives lies the answer. Dunbar's life subsequently spiraled downward. She was in a serious automobile accident that damaged her body and her looks. She was sued by a former patient, a Maytag heiress. One of her close friends, a one-time patient, committed suicide under peculiar circumstances. Her live-in male companion committed suicide. She had trouble with alcohol, and died in 1959 at the much-too-young-age of 57. Her daughter found her in her basement swimming pool under circumstances that were unclear.

The College of Pastoral Supervision and Psychotherapy began granting an annual "Helen Flanders Dunbar Award" in 2002 for significant achievements in the field of clinical pastoral supervision. Dunbar's only child, Marcia Dunbar-Soule Dobson, is a psychotherapist now working in Colorado. She participated in the inauguration of that award.

In retrospect Dunbar must be seen as essential to the success of the Boisen movement in its early decades. Without her, the clinical training movement would almost certainly have devolved and degraded into a program of skills training and didactic programs. It would almost certainly have entirely divested itself of its alliance with psychoanalytic theory of any variety, and certainly that of the Freudian tradition.

Before and after Dunbar the Council was engaged in a two-front war, with the Cabot group on the one hand and the larger Protestant public on the other. On both fronts the name of Freud stirred up fear and loathing. Dunbar, as a psychiatrist and a sexually liberated woman as well, was simply not going to survive among a group of typical Protestant clergy for very long, especially with the followers of Cabot attacking her flank. The wonder is that she lasted as long as she did and was as monumentally effective as she was. But then, her moniker was Minerva.

3.
THE EMERGENCE OF SEWARD HILTNER

If Helen Flanders Dunbar was the person who put Boisen on the map, launching his mission to the Protestant denominations, it was Seward Hiltner who later gave the Boisen movement theological respectability. Though theologically trained, Dunbar was principally a psychiatrist. Hiltner was principally a pastoral theologian, and not only a pastoral theologian but also arguably the best in the country in his prime, in the mid-20th century. From his chair at Princeton Theological Seminary he was the preeminent voice providing clinical pastoral training within a strong and essential theological structure. As Porter French wrote, Hiltner was "our Lenin."[5] Like Lenin, he certainly gave ideological respectability to a ragtag movement. Hiltner helped stanch the bleeding in the clinical pastoral community that resulted from the Freudian influence, and more especially the influence of Reich. In the early 1940s the Council lost a large foundation grant, the bulk of its funds for reasons not known, but it would be a good guess that the withdrawal of funds had something to do with Dunbar's links with the psychoanalytic movement, and perhaps even specifically with Reich. It was no secret that her front man, Robert Brinkman, was a Reichian. Hiltner may well have concurred entirely with Dunbar personally, but if so he was a more careful politician. Certainly Hiltner himself was very much a Freudian, but as an academic he was somewhat inoculated from such charges and able to slip under the public-relations radar on that issue. He could easily distance himself from philosophies that frighten the natives simply on the grounds of scholarship. Studying Freud doesn't always stretch to "being a Freudian." Dunbar, in her leadership of the Council, had no such cover. From the 1940s onward, psychoanalytic thinking was expunged gradually from the Boisen movement, though at a snail's pace. But those clinical supervisors who were known to be Reichian were threatened with summary expulsion. In the late 1940s at least one, and likely others, were deprived of their Council credentials because of their promotion of Reichian therapy.

After Boisen moved to Chicago, essentially abdicating his broad leadership role in the new clinical pastoral training movement embodied in the Council, Dunbar seized the reins of power. In 1935, she appointed Hiltner to the position of Executive Secretary. He was young, bright, and male, and he filled that role from 1935 until 1938. He had good bona fides: He had been trained first by Boisen at Elgin State Hospital in Chicago and subsequently by Carroll Wise at Worcester.

Though Hiltner never functioned as a clinical pastoral supervisor as such, he was certified and was competent enough to function in that capacity. All indications are that he did a competent job as the Council's Executive, but it is also said that he chafed under Dunbar's directives. He reported in a 1975 article in the *Journal of Pastoral Care* that he had virtually to defy Dunbar in order to go to Cincinnati to meet with and compare notes with Joseph Fletcher.[6] Fletcher was an academic and a clinical pastoral giant, but for whatever reason was never embraced by, or perhaps was never interested in, the Council's or the Institute's certification credential. Hiltner felt, undoubtedly correctly, that such division among clinicians was more a matter of personalities than of substantive issues. Whatever else he was, Fletcher was certainly an able pastoral clinician and a leader in the field.

Having his office in Dunbar's apartment, in a converted maid's room, was almost certainly a bit confining for Hiltner, which was essentially living with one's boss. There was also gossip that Dunbar and Hiltner were at one point lovers, which would not be shocking to anyone who knew them both. Such a complicated relationship would have been difficult to sustain over a long period of time, with or without a sexual connection. In any case, Hiltner resigned in 1938 to become executive secretary for the Commission on Religion and Health in the Federal Council of Churches of Christ. From there he went in the 1950s to earn his Ph.D., and finally to teach in the Divinity School at the University of Chicago. He was simultaneously visiting professor at the Menninger School of Psychiatry, in Topeka. In 1961, he was appointed Professor of Theology and Personality at Princeton Theological Seminary where he remained until his death in 1984, having officially retired in 1980.

As an academic and a writer Hiltner helped define who Boisen was, drawing in part from his personal experience of him as his clinical pastoral supervisor. He reported that Boisen was less interested in training as such, and more interested in exploring persons' illnesses, in the hope for healing. Boisen functioned more as a self-appointed psychotherapist or psychoanalyst than as a teacher, although he was always eager to attract those who would want to learn from him. Hiltner assessed Boisen as "a Harnack-Schweitzer type of liberal with a cautious but deeply felt mysticism." He also assessed Boisen as an inflexible moralistic American—towards himself, but not toward others. That rigidity seems to have been directed toward sexual issues. But Hiltner saw Boisen as one who had fully absorbed the dynamic insights of Freud. This is about as brilliant and insightful a synopsis of Boisen as anyone has offered.[7]

One of the notable projects that Hiltner spawned in New York was the creation of the New York Psychology Group. This was an informal discussion group he convened in the war years of the 1940s, consisting of Paul Tillich, Ruth Benedict, Eric Fromm, Rollo May, David Roberts, Carl Rogers, Frances Wickes, and a variety of other luminaries—psychoanalysts, anthropologists, and theologians. This group gained serious notoriety. Its focus was the boundary between psychology and religion. Probably no one but Hiltner, with his charm, status, and location could have pulled together such a substantive group over a period of several years.

Hiltner was a giant figure in the clinical pastoral movement throughout his professional life, yet he remained all his life on the boundary between the clinical and the academic. Although he was principally an academic, Hiltner remained consistently an astute clinician, according to his last Ph.D. student, Brian Childs. His teaching was rooted in the clinical, and the competition to study under him was fierce. He was very progressive, and he strongly promoted the interface of religion with psychoanalytic theory and practice. Hiltner was arguably more effective than any pastoral clinician in asserting the compatibility of pastoral training with psychoanalytic theory. His writings on the role of the pastor provided the substantive theoretical and practical support for seminarians in the U.S. in the mid-20th century.

In the 1940s and 1950s, Hiltner was also considered to be, in spite of his academic perch, the closest thing to the principal voice for the clinical pastoral movement generally, in all its iterations. With that unofficial authority, he was able to convene the leadership of the various competing clinical pastoral groups in 1944 and urge them to start talking to one another. That nudge was ultimately effective, but it took another 24 years before there was a meeting of minds, in the form of the 1967 federation, the formation of the Association for Clinical Pastoral Education. Hiltner became disenchanted with the federation and dismayed by the fruit of his labor by the time he died 17 years later. That the federation developed poorly was not the responsibility of Hiltner. He was merely the one who goaded the disparate groups into talking with and relating to one another.

Hiltner sought to encourage religious leaders to engage the secular world. When the first of two famous Kinsey Reports, *Sexual Behavior in the Human Male,* was published in 1948 and its sequel on the female in 1952, it was arguably the first shot fired in the soon-to-come Sexual Revolution. The reports revealed a lot of data that were shocking to middle-class Americans. It revealed that there was a lot more non-marital sexual contact taking place than most anyone wanted to acknowledge. Half of the males reported extramarital sexual experience at some point in their lives, and some lesser percentage of women reported similar experiences. Forty-six percent of males reported having "reacted" sexually to a person of the same sex sometime in the course of their adult lives, and about 11 percent of white males considered themselves bisexual. The Kinsey Reports were a culture shock in the post-World War II period.

It is no small irony that Kinsey's laboratory was situated in the same University of Indiana, in Bloomington, where Boisen's father and progenitors taught. Kinsey could have walked over to Boisen's childhood home. The ghosts there might have told him a lot about sex.

While Kinsey became a household word, the educated leadership in the American religious community seemed rendered mute by the Kinsey data. Very little serious religious commentary followed the Reports. And this was in spite of the fact that Kinsey's data revealed there was a very wide gap between typical American sexual behavior and the proper behavior that was taught by the religious communities. As a college student in those years heading for the ministry, I recall being personally troubled by and negatively reactive to the Kinsey Reports. I was a child of my time. In 1953, a woman "expert" of some sort came to my college, Randolph-Macon in Virginia, and spoke of how the newly invented birth control pills were going to change American sexual ethics. This speech unnerved me. Little did I know how correct she was. I wish I could remember her name.

To his credit, Seward Hiltner weighed in on Kinsey where others feared to tread. He wrote a 1953 monograph for the National Board of the YMCA entitled *Sex Ethics and the Kinsey Report*. Now, more than a half-century later and on the other side of the Sexual Revolution, the Hiltner book seems quaint and very cautious. But Hiltner deserves great credit for a willingness to face the sexual music publicly as a prominent religious leader and scholar. Apparently, no one else had such nerve.

The first thing Hiltner noted was that the books themselves seemed to be "the most unread best-sellers of all time." He surmised that readers simply looked up themselves and then closed the book. Hiltner's thesis was that Kinsey should be commended for exposing the actual nature of sexual life in the American community. He followed up with a secondary argument, that current sexual behavior in general was not congruent with the alleged Christian view of sex. Hiltner commended Kinsey for this exposition of reality pertaining to sexual life in the U.S.

In his own work, however, Hiltner trapped himself somewhat by his repeated references to "the Christian view of sex." In other places he assured the reader, contradictorily, that there is a variety of Christian views of sex. But he never makes clear exactly what the parameters of that variety might be. And there was, in fact, no agreement among the various Christian groups on what "the Christian view of sex" might be. With Catholic monastics on the one side, sexually liberated groups like the Unitarians on the other, and numerous variations in-between, there was no way one could clearly communicate "a Christian view of sex," except to say that the great majority were sexually repressive. Hiltner muffed that issue.

On the other hand, Hiltner might have stated boldly that the Christian view of sex is that sex should occur only in marriage, and for Catholic Christians specifically, only for purposes of procreation in marriage. But as an identified Presbyterian Christian, Hiltner likely would not have wanted to open the question of whether he might be a dissenter from the Presbyterian position. Had he done so, he likely would have never been appointed to the faculty of the preeminent Presbyterian Theological Seminary at Princeton.

Hiltner also attempted to take a cautiously liberal posture in response to Kinsey's statistics on homosexuality. While he concurred with the Christian and Presbyterian tradition that fixed homosexuality as both wrong and unnatural, he took a relaxed stance regarding casual adolescent homosexual exploration, referring to it as a matter of no consequence. In all fairness to Hiltner, there was no way he could have kept his prestigious university teaching positions as a Christian theologian and publicly supported Kinsey's work unequivocally. Hiltner's book was at once an act of both bravery and cowardice. If it was ultimately a failure, it was brave of him to write candidly on a very taboo and dangerous subject while most religious scholars remained mute, or repeated the party line. He failed to assert strongly enough what he knew as a scholar deeply immersed in Freud, that sexuality is the most problematic of all human experiences, and that the customary denial and repression lead to no good end. But it must be noted that in that era sexual behavior was simply not discussed at all publicly or in polite company.

The Sexual Revolution that was only about a decade away would solve Hiltner's dilemma and at the same time make his book irrelevant, though it remains a very interesting artifact of history.

On a personal level, Hiltner had a sotto voce reputation in the clinical pastoral world of being a hard drinker, an obsessive smoker, and a daring lover of women. He was not unique in that respect. These kinds of behaviors were a virtual badge of honor among pastoral clinicians, as well as many academicians, if not the mainstream religious.

Hiltner reported in his 1975 article in the *Journal of Pastoral Care*, "Fifty Years of Learning," that he was generally disappointed in the clinical training movement. He felt that it had been successful on the clinical and practical side, but was theoretically and theologically uninteresting and unsophisticated. He felt that Europeans would be justified ultimately in judging American clinical training to be philosophically lightweight. The subsequent decades were to prove Hiltner to be prophetic.

In the mid-1970s, in my one personal encounter with Hiltner, at the Institute of Religion in Houston, he had just read my controversial 1975 article, "Toward a More Flexible Monogamy," published first in *Christianity and Crisis*. He praised me for it, and we engaged in an extended friendly conversation. He encouraged me to keep writing. As we parted in the halls of the Institute, he wished me well, and patted me on my buttocks. I took that gesture of familiarity to be a strong patriarchal and sensuous blessing, and I greatly appreciated it. He died a few years later in 1984 at the age of 74. Hiltner was a giant in his time.

4.
THE LEGACY OF RUSSELL L. DICKS

Russell Dicks, along with Philip Guiles, became Richard Cabot's two principal lieutenants after the 1930 alienation from Boisen and Dunbar and the cooling of his affection for the Council. Dicks did his clinical training at Worcester Hospital under Carroll Wise. However, Dicks had little interest in the unconscious life of either the patient, the pastor, or—seemingly—himself. He did not bond with Wise. He therefore joined Cabot's unofficial dissident group, first called "The Cabot Club," and then "The New England Theological Schools Committee on Clinical Training," and which finally in 1944 morphed into the "Institute for Pastoral Care," commonly known as "The Institute." This tradition started out as strongly anti-psychological, and more especially anti-Freudian, reflecting the personal views of Cabot himself, who mocked psychiatry as "sick-a-try." And it persevered in its adversarial relationship with the leadership of the Council. Dicks thus became an early key leader of that small dissident group headed by Cabot. Oddly, Cabot remained president of the Council until 1935.

Cabot became attracted to Dicks, and said so explicitly, when he discovered that Dicks was transcribing the extemporaneous prayers that he created and delivered to hospital patients. "He writes down his own prayers!" exclaimed a jubilant Cabot. This was the kind of comfort Cabot considered appropriate for a chaplain to provide a patient. The contrast between Boisen and Dicks on this matter is quite stark. For Boisen, the critical material was what the patient was able to say, not what the chaplain had to say. A prayer said by a chaplain may be a work of art, and worthy of memorializing, and indeed comforting, but it did little or nothing to explicate the riddle of the suffering patient. Nothing better illustrates the contrast between Boisen's approach to patients and Cabot's notion of what chaplains ought to be doing. This also sheds light on why Boisen favored psychiatric hospitals as training sites, and Cabot preferred general hospitals only, preferences which were acted out in subsequent decades by the two major certifying groups, the Council and the Institute. General hospital patients are usually hospitalized briefly. Psychiatric patients are generally in for an extended stay. Building a pastoral and therapeutic relationship is much more likely with the latter. And from Cabot's perspective, there was nothing to be done for psychiatric patients except to warehouse them, until such a time as a curative drug could be found.

Dicks resigned from the Council in 1935, the same year Cabot was removed as President. But he remained with Cabot's New England group. He resigned from that group too, in 1938. Then he returned to the Council in 1956, apparently to support his directorship of a clinical training program at Duke University Hospital. Then he resigned again the next year. He died in 1965 while serving at the Orlando Pastoral Counseling Center. He was only 59.

Dicks was a prolific writer, authoring some 15 books, and a key player in the early years of the clinical pastoral movement; but he was consistently allied philosophically with Cabot against Boisen. Dicks' most prominent book, jointly authored with Cabot, was *The Art of Ministering to the Sick*. The book presented a chaplaincy role that was top heavy. That is to say, Dicks and Cabot focused on all the things chaplains can do for a patient, such as praying, Bible reading, exhorting, encouraging, and so forth. The pastoral role as presented is a grab bag of action. There is one chapter entitled "Listening" in which the authors come as close as they ever do to Boisen's therapeutic approach. Two kinds of listening are described. First there is directed listening in which the patient is instructed to talk about particular matters. Then there is passive listening, described as simply following the patient wherever the patient wants to go. This almost links up with the Boisen approach to patient care. But it is only close. To put it boldly, Dicks and Cabot viewed listening as a quiet interlude between such initiatives from the chaplain as prayer, instruction, encouragement, and the like. There is really little common ground between Dicks and Boisen. Boisen would certainly have leveled a charge against Dicks and Cabot of "pastoral treatment without diagnosis." The index in the book reveals no mention of either Boisen or Freud. The contrast between this book and Boisen's *Exploration of the Inner World* could not be starker. Both books were published in the same year, 1936.

The reason for Dicks' resignation from the Council in 1935 and the New England group in 1938 is not known. Gossip held that Dicks resigned from the Council in 1957 because of sexual accusations regarding a relationship with a woman at Duke. Each of his three resignations may have been related to his sexual behavior. E. Brooks Holifield seems to support such a surmise when he reports that Dicks resigned from the Institute (actually at that time called The New England Group) in 1938 because of a disagreement with Cabot "about moral conduct."[8] That seems likely to have been a veiled reference to sexual conduct. According to oral tradition, Dicks was the most unabashedly liberated of all sexually liberated pastoral clinicians in the early years. He traveled a great deal, lecturing and teaching, and is reputed to have appeared at meetings with a wide variety of women on his arm. In the lingo of later days, Dicks was said to be an avid womanizer. But as was typical of Dicks' own era, no one dared discuss openly a matter of countercultural sexual behavior, even when it was obvious. Think of John Kennedy or Paul Tillich. In that pre-Sexual Revolution era, this was another case of "the emperor's new clothes." Dicks lived during the right time. Had he lived another decade or two, he would have been pilloried.

I interviewed Dicks' widow at their home in Bonner Elk, North Carolina, on October 16, 1993, 28 years after his death. She graciously welcomed me as an overnight guest and allowed me to examine what was left of Dicks' papers, a sparse collection. I did not find anything that was new or notable. I wasn't callous enough, or daring enough—which is it?—to ask her directly about his sexual history. She did voluntarily disclose to me "he was always away and never home." I thought that she was communicating something by that.

In 1952 (the year I graduated from high school), S.A. Lewin, M.D., and John Gilmore, Ph.D., published a quaint little book entitled *Sex After Forty*.[9] The book provided very directive instructions on how to enjoy sexual relations, explicitly after age 40, but implicitly at any age. The book characterizes the forties as the turbulent years because of the onset of menopause. The book presented a number of cases of problem marriages that were solved by the authors through direct advice and instruction on how to be a more effective sexual partner. The book has all the flavor of an instruction manual or a sexual cookbook. It was directed obviously to middle-class people who were more or less inhibited or ignorant of basic, elementary sexual knowledge and skill. The book seemed to be implicitly addressing assumptions that sexual relations are expected to terminate at the onset of menopause. The focus was entirely on marital sex. No issues of extramarital sex, premarital sex, homosexuality, or masturbation are mentioned. The book does not explore sexual ethics in any sense. It focuses on physiology and is directed toward the physical sexual practices of the inhibited and the poorly informed on matters of sexuality and the body, and on how to achieve a satisfactory sexual experience. Implicitly, but not explicitly, the book was directed at the frustrated married. The posture of the therapeutic treatment is mostly behavior modification by way of direct instruction. The solutions seem quite simple and often quaint. The book posits in the reader extraordinary biological ignorance on matters of human sexuality.

Curiously, Russell Dicks was asked to write the Introduction. He is identified as chaplain at Duke University Hospital. The reason for his being invited to do so is not explained and is a bit mysterious. He must have been known then as some kind of underground sex expert. And he does agree with the authors that sex after 40 is a serious social problem that needed addressing. In his Introduction he writes rather dramatically, "The stormy forties and later life have been clouded in mystery, in anxiety and dread.

Sex After Forty is a shaft of sunshine through this heavy cloud." He seems to assume that the reader will think that sexual pleasure ends with menopause. If I myself had read the book the year it was published, when I was 18, as yet bereft of any sexual experience outside of myself, even then I would have considered the book rather elementary, even puerile.

In the first paragraph of Dicks' 2000-word Introduction he makes a rather startling claim that must be purposely hyperbolic. He writes:[10]

> Sex was discovered in our generation. By that I mean sex as a potent force for happiness in human living is only now being released from the fears, taboos, restrictions and guilt complexes that have made of sex a destructive rather than the potentially wonderful creative force that it actually is; and when I say 'creative' I am not speaking of the reproduction of the race.

Dicks was of course overreaching. The lady doth protest too much, methinks. Is it possible that he had forgotten the biblical Song of Songs? Furthermore, artistic reproductions of explicit and ecstatic sexual pleasure can be found in many cultures over many centuries. Think also of *Carmina Burana,* preserved for centuries in a medieval monastery.

Dicks here seems to be making a clarion call with an uncertain trumpet. He alludes to some sort of new age in relation to sex, an age without fears, taboos, restrictions, and guilt; an age of sexual pleasure without the requirement of procreation. We must conjecture that he is simply making a comparison between his generation and the rather more timid sexuality of the Victorian era—if we can believe the doubtful claim that they were as timid as they pretended to be. Or perhaps Dicks is covertly drawing a vivid contrast between his own earlier life and his newly discovered sexual freedom.

Dicks goes on to argue that only in the current generation has it been possible for young people to have information about the sexual side of their natures and to manage intelligently one of the strongest forces in their lives. But what that new kind of management would look like he does not make clear.

Dicks does not engage in discussions of sexual ethics as such, but he does leave some hints. He claims, "Sex After Forty marks a definite advance in the struggle of the human creature to gain freedom from Puritanical tyranny." But in fact the book only discusses physical sexual problems within a conventional marriage. And curiously, Dicks himself earlier recommended in a review published in the journal *Pastoral Psychology* that such books as this one be sold only to persons approved by their pastors or physicians. Go figure.

Dicks seems passionate about the need for sex education in the public arena, with some reservations. He makes the stunning hyperbolic charge that for clergy to bless marriages without prior sex education "is like placing loaded pistols in the hands of children and assuring them that they were playing with harmless toys." Only an intense personal passion could have led Dicks to construct such a bizarre metaphor.

The only sentence in which either Dicks or the book itself makes mention of non-marital sex is also a curious one. Dicks writes: "I would consider it less a sin to give my blessing to a woman who had had excessive pre-marital sexual experience than to a girl entering marriage without pre-marital sexual instruction."[11] Thus, Dicks is clear that he passionately promoted sexual pleasure, and that he is more concerned about that than he is about non-marital sex. But beyond this hint of Dicks' sexual libertarianism, neither he nor the book give further clues about his or the authors' general philosophy or ethics of sexual behavior.

Cabot had been especially impressed by Dicks because he took a pastoral stance focused more on the conscious mind of the patient as distinct from Boisen's focus on the unconscious. And Cabot was very favorably impressed with Dick's aggressive use of prayer with patients. Dicks' approach was not Boisen's, whose objective was to invite the patient to relate his own story, and particularly his own pathology. Because Cabot objected to Boisen's exploratory in-depth therapeutic approach to patients and his psychoanalytically informed philosophy of pastoral care and counseling, Dicks' directive and instructive posture with patients suited Cabot well. Dicks and Cabot co-authored *The Art of Ministering to the Sick*. But none of this background sheds light on why Dicks was prefacing a book on the skills required for satisfactory postmenopausal sexual activity. One has to conjecture that Dicks' reputation as sexual libertarian ahead of his time was part of the equation and the likely motivation.

Dicks' anti-psychology, and especially his anti-Freudian posture, and his focus on pastoral training as a skill-focused undertaking gained preeminence—even if he personally did not—in the decades subsequent to the federation of all training organizations in 1967. In the movement at large, Dicks' philosophy of clinical training ultimately trumped that of Boisen's.

5.
THE FIRST QUARTER CENTURY

As Boisen moved to Chicago and abandoned the leadership of the Council that he had inaugurated, he set himself adrift from the decision makers in the clinical training movement. His newly created Chicago Council for Clinical Pastoral Training seems not to have gone anywhere. Of course, Boisen had no Dunbar to make such an organization work.

As the clinical training movement moved into its second decade, several countervailing trends emerged. Foremost, the anti-psychiatry axis, which was particularly anti-Freudian, prospered by way of the Cabot Club. Cabot referred to psychiatry as "sick-a-try." And Cabot initially carried several of the key Boston area chaplains with him, Carroll Wise being a notable and distinguished exception. The anti-psychiatry subgroup continued to consider Boisen a lost cause, someone with an organic brain syndrome (Cabot's diagnosis) who was incurable. That perspective dominated the Cabot circle until 1939, when Cabot died. Subsequently, something of an openness developed among the Cabot partisans for an appreciation of psychiatry in general, but it manifested itself in a partiality for Jung as opposed to Freud. Jung believed in God—or the gods—and was less attentive to the human struggle with sexuality, which endeared him to the typically religious. Freud was popularly considered obsessed with sex, and was a declared atheist. As a religious believer and as someone not eager to focus deeply on issues of sexuality, Jung naturally was attractive to the more traditionally religious. Furthermore, Jung believed that the gods communicated with human beings in their dreams and visions. That was also gratifying, but about as unclinical a position as could be taken. And no one seemed to notice that Jung's religious interests had little or no connection with Christianity. Nor did they notice that Jung was favorably disposed to Nazism, and in fact in close personal contact with key Nazi leaders, most notably Herman Goering. But Jung was interested in the gods, and that was what mattered, especially in comparison to Freud, the atheist.

The real irony of all this preference for Jung over Freud in the religious community was the fact that Jung was, in later American lingo, a serious sexual boundary violator. However, the American Jungians never seemed to notice this. And on the other hand, Freud's own personal sexual behavior would have put him right at home ethically in any conservative American church. Two notable biographers of Freud, Peter Gay and Elizabeth Roudinesco, conclude that Freud never had an extramarital relationship in his life. It seems that even the most conventional American Christians would have embraced such a standard of sexual behavior. I take a slightly contrary position on Freud's sexual life, but my dissent does not change in any significant way the conservative picture of Freud's sexual life. No one disputes that Freud, unlike most therapists of the time, assiduously avoided sexual contact with patients and was not known to have lovers. Freud himself confessed that sexual relations with Martha, his wife, ceased after the birth of their last child. He referred to himself as living a celibate life.

Some scholars contend, however, that Freud was sexually involved with his sister-in-law, Minna, his wife's younger, unmarried, and more attractive sister, whose fiancé died just prior to their wedding. Minna lived with the Freud family for the rest of her life. Her bedroom was adjacent to the master bedroom. Curiously, Minna was known to answer the phone as if she was Freud's wife, "Frau Professor Freud," perhaps communicating obliquely or unconsciously her actual feelings. Unlike Martha, Minna was Freud's intellectual equal; she was conversant with Freud on the subject of psychoanalytic theory and practice. Martha, on the other hand, was all "kitchen and nursery." Furthermore, Martha had the notion that her husband's work was somehow pornographic. Nor is there dispute about the fact that Freud and Minna sometimes vacationed together, touring Europe or taking the baths, as was the custom in that era. Some scholars infer from the account of Freud's selling some valuable books to pay for some vague medical treatment for Minna was actually an abortion. And then a group of letters from a certain time when Freud was likely to have corresponded with Minna is missing, likely to have been purposely removed and disposed of. It is also seems clear that Freud continued to be interested in sex, but that his sexual connection with Martha was less than fulfilling. The data is murky and the source is, of course, Freud himself.[12]

Settling the question of the nature of Freud's relationship with Minna is an unlikely prospect. That Freud was, in his own words celibate, however, should not be taken too literally. He was certainly at least celibate except for his sister-in-law. Freud after all believed in sexual liberation, confessing that he liberated many but benefited little himself. That little may have been Minna. Furthermore, Freud's Jewish roots—even if he were not observant—would have had some influence on his actions and his ethics. Jews of Eastern Europe and Spain, of the Sephardic tradition, practiced polygamy (and still do), and Freud would certainly have known that. Taking a wife's sister for a second wife would have had no moral stigma in Sephardic Judaism, and only the slightest stigma in Ashkenazi Judaism.[13] Of course, the ambient Catholic culture of Austria would have pilloried Freud, or worse, had such a relationship been disclosed: all the more reason for Freud to declare himself celibate. Thus, I dissent from the conclusions of the esteemed biographers of Freud, Peter Gay and Elizabeth Roudinesco, and place my bet, as Jung and a number of historians and biographers have, that Sigmund and Minna were a sexual pair. But does it really make any difference either way?

The above digression may seem like a detour, but in fact it is not. Issues of sexuality burned hot in the first generation of the clinical pastoral movement. While Boisen himself was severely restrained sexually, most of his followers were quite the opposite, a pattern replicated in the clinical pastoral movement. Even those in the Cabot camp who had no use for Freud whatsoever were often known to be sexual libertarians, Russell Dicks being the preeminent example.

The proxy conflict between Cabot and Boisen—and it was proxy simply because Boisen had no interest in a fight—also pertained to the status of the chaplain in medical institutions. Cabot viewed the chaplain as the helpmeet to the real therapist, the physician. Boisen viewed the chaplain as an authentic psychotherapist in his or her own right.

Cabot also had an investment in training programs situated exclusively in general hospitals. He saw no benefit in attempting work with psychologically disturbed patients. He was convinced that their problems were chemical. Boisen on the other hand was primarily interested in psychiatric hospitals where he could engage patients in depth over a significant period of time—patients like the one he himself had been and would again be in the future. For Boisen, the visions and delusions of emotionally disturbed persons were a doorway to the meaning of their disturbance. Certainly he should know.

There was another aspect of the Boisen-Cabot struggle that must be noted. Cabot saw clinical training as education, that is, learning how to assist patients on a conscious level and how to prepare the way for the true healers, the physicians. For Boisen, clinical training was as much a matter of the development of the chaplain himself as it was a matter of skills development. Or more so. In other words, the person of the chaplain was more critical in the psychotherapeutic task than the skills he or she might develop. The chaplain then for Boisen played a therapeutic role in relation to the patient. For Cabot, the chaplain was a helpmeet for the authentic therapist, the physician. This conflict between Boisen and Cabot was deep and was not destined to end well.

The Boston group that pulled away from Boisen and linked up with Cabot as the Cabot Club eventually took the moniker, the New England Theological Schools Committee on Clinical Training. Its method was more didactic than the Council's, which was more process-oriented. The New England group's clinical training programs generally consisted of a great number of lectures and much reading. The Council's principal mode of teaching was reviewing clinical cases among peers and reflecting on the relationships among the peers, with the assistance of a clinical supervisor. The New England group was more deeply in bed with the seminaries and, in particular, their teaching modality. Thus the seminaries were generally more comfortable with them. All this led to the New England group as a more conventional organization, and the Council as a more radical one. The Council was made up of persons, many who preferred to think outside the box as they engaged in "training." The New England group was generally much more conventional and took a traditional view of "education." It is hard to envision any Cabot-oriented supervisor dabbling with Reich's radical orgone therapy, for example. But some of the Council supervisors did, and they continued to do so even after Reich was officially proscribed. The most notable difference between the New England group and the Council was that one was led by a rational and reputable physician, and the other was led by an occasionally psychotic minister. That made a great difference to many.

In the internecine conflict, the first gambit was to accuse the Council of sexual improprieties. It is true that a great many supervisors were flouting conventional sexual ethics. But then so were some of the key Institute leaders, if one can believe gossip in either case. No authority in either subgroup was more of what the later feminists were fond of labeling "a womanizer" than Russell Dicks. None of this entered the scholarly discourse, but it was widely known and discussed.

So sex became a real "red herring." The Council was considered sexually adventuresome, and the Institute was considered morally proper by middle-class standards. But the fact is that in both camps individuals were all over the map. Sexual behavior was mostly kept private, especially in those days prior to electronic communication, and few were confessing their sins openly. Both sides were playing a game of "gotcha."

With Robert Brinkman as Executive Secretary (appointed in 1938), the Council fell out of favor with a major financial supporter, The Whitney Foundation. Their annual funding was withdrawn in 1942. Richard Lehman implied in an unpublished paper, "Some Footnotes on a Glorious Tradition," that the cause was Brinkman's sexual acting out.[14] However, any number of issues might have spooked an established benefactor like Whitney. In any case, it was not Brinkman who was ousted in that year, but Dunbar herself. Brinkman kept his leadership position for another four years. He resigned in 1946 to become a private practice psychoanalyst. He was a Reichian, having been introduced to Reich by Dunbar's first husband, Theodore Wolf. Fred Kuether replaced Brinkman as Executive Secretary of the Council in 1947.

Furthermore, Lehman also describes the 1948 annual conference of the Council held in Perkiomen, Pennsylvania. He writes that "a new low of acting out by some of the supervisors led several people to action." While he does not specify what kind of acting out he refers to, a substantive guess would be sexual. Lehman says that a number of meetings were held in the East "to get them [the Council] back on track with more responsible behavior."[15] Lehman says the efforts paid off well. He gave credit to Reuel Howe, Tom Brigham, Ernest Bruner, Otis Rice, and Executive Director Kuether.

I visited with Lehman personally in the last decade of the century and found him to be a good-hearted guy, who can probably be trusted with the history that he relates. His references to "acting out," however, particularly in reference to Brinkman, are arguably a misuse of the psychoanalytic category. "Acting out" implies behavior that is driven by unconscious forces outside one's awareness. Not every instance of unconventional sexual activity can be labeled "acting out." Brinkman as a Reichian was undoubtedly liberated sexually, yet no evidence exists that he "acted out" in that respect. But Lehman was a key Institute supervisor, which meant that he was likely somewhat biased against Council supervisors and particularly reactive to their reputation for sexual freedom. He must have been an Institute guest at the Council gathering at Perkiomen.

Reuel Howe, according to Lehman, the putative leader who put down the Reichians and perhaps others who were said to be "acting out," was renowned for his book, *The Miracle of Dialogue*. The gossip about Howe, who was a professor at Virginia Theological Seminary, in Alexandria, was that he could talk for hours about the wonder of dialogue but was completely inept at engaging in it. An examination of his very popular book will find no mention of Freud or the psychoanalytic contribution to clinical training, or even of Boisen himself. Howe seems to be making the point that the beneficial fruits of clinical pastoral training were theological rather than psychological. Such juxtaposition is arbitrary, compartmentalized, and quite misleading. But Howe did bequeath to the future a stirring and widely used rant about what he as a professor anticipated that his seminarians might experience in clinical training:[16]

> I want [the students] "dunked"—plunged deeply into life, brought up grasping and dripping, and returned to us humble and ready to learn. Until all students are faced with the tragedies, the contradictions, and the stark questions of life, they cannot understand the need for redemption or God's redemptive action. I want my students to lose, as soon as possible, their easy faith, their ready answers; and I want them to lose any hope of ever again having an easy faith or a ready answer. I want them to lose their personal conceits and their illusions about themselves, their illusions about their fellow men and their illusions about God. I want their assumptions about ministry and their assumptions about how they are going to conduct their ministry completely destroyed.

The quarter century since Boisen began clinical pastoral training at Worcester State ended in considerable organizational disarray. On the one hand, the American Protestant churches were highly favorable toward clinical pastoral training, making it virtually a universal requirement for their seminarians. On the other hand, there was wide divergence of opinion as to what exactly clinical training was supposed to be. The Lutherans and the Southern Baptists moved to establish their own denominational certifying bodies that would credential supervisors in-house, so to speak. For the Lutherans this strategy would circumvent any alien ideology, such as that from Freud or Reich, or any ideology that threatened to contaminate their pastors. One might assume that for the most part, the covert agenda was to keep their young ministers from reading Sigmund Freud. For the Southern Baptists, their motivation was to escape the bureaucratic tyranny of both the Council and the Institute. And in a curious and profound twist, the Southern Baptists were evangelistic in their promotion of Freud and a psychoanalytic approach to training. The two preeminent Southern Baptist clinical pastoral supervisors were Wayne Oates and Myron Madden. For each of them Freud's theories were inextricably linked to effective clinical training and to effective pastoral care and counseling. Both were profoundly shaped by psychoanalytic theory and practice. But neither Oates nor Madden were much at home in the Southern Baptist Convention. They existed on the outer fringe of the Baptists. When Madden gave Oates' eulogy at his 1999 funeral, he said of him that "he came unto his own, and his own received him not." Both Oates and Madden were strong and richly endowed ministers, but they were most atypical Southern Baptists.

The chaos and fragmentation of the clinical pastoral movement in its first quarter century began to be addressed by Seward Hiltner. In 1944, just as the New England group officially renamed itself the Institute for Pastoral Care, Hiltner called together all the disparate clinical pastoral groups for discussions. This was the first call for a coming together of the entire clinical pastoral movement since the 1930 split between Cabot and Boisen. Almost as many deans and seminary professors attended this meeting as clinical supervisors. There clearly was interest in some kind of unity. However, it was also clear, according to Ed Thornton, that there was a preference among the academicians for the posture of the Boston group, the Institute. Hiltner spoke at the conclusion of the meeting to say "we will not have complete uniformity or organic union within the clinical pastoral movement ... but that cooperative relationships must be maintained now that they have been established."[17] Twenty-three years later an organic union would in fact take place, for good or for ill. Data suggests Hiltner did support organic union at that time.

It is remarkable that there were only about 30 training centers of any sort in 1944, and most of them were with the Council.[18] The Boisen movement grew from the four training centers Boisen had spawned in 1930 to 30 in 1944. The subsequent two decades were to be a time of significantly greater expansion.

6.
THE TOWER OF BABEL REDUX

With the dismissal of Dunbar, Cabot dead, and Boisen's lack of interest in organizational issues, the entire clinical pastoral field was in flux in the 1940s. After Dunbar was dismissed in 1942, her associate, Robert Brinkman, assumed command of the Council. Brinkman made Fred Kuether his associate. But there was no preeminent leader emerging from the crowd to assume leadership of the entire movement. Seward Hiltner had moved to fill the vacuum, but he was identified as an academic, not as a clinician.

Boisen himself during this period was troubled by the increasing libertinism in the movement. As sexually inhibited as he was, he could not possibly have been comfortable with sexual freedom, and the Reichians must certainly have severely rattled him. But while many pastoral clinicians, especially those of the Institute, gravitated to the psychology of Jung because of Jung's minimization of sexual issues, Boisen remained true to the man whose writings saved him during his first hospitalization, Freud.

In the middle 1940s, there began some pushback against Robert Brinkman, the Council's Executive. This pushback was dramatized in the above-mentioned Perkiomen meeting of the Council. Brinkman would have difficulty filling Dunbar's earlier charismatic leadership role at the Council. A major liability for Brinkman politically was that he was a Reichian. With negative thinking about psychoanalytic thought escalating, the negativity toward Reich was especially strong. Brinkman resigned in 1946 to go into private practice as a psychotherapist. Though certainly not a Reichian himself, Ed Thornton makes a point of praising Brinkman strongly for both his character and skill. This was a remarkable tribute from an Institute man for a Reichian leader of the Council.[19]

> Brinkman was well-liked as a supervisor. He was discreet concerning his private life, but sensitive toward others and careful not to offend them. He had an emancipated attitude toward conventional standards, but he was never dogmatic about his liberated views, nor did he impose his own values on others.

Thornton added that Brinkman, though a Reichian, at no time allowed the Council to become explicitly identified with any particular psychoanalytic or theological school of thought."

That was clearly high praise from Thornton, whose certification and loyalty was with the Institute and therefore could not be presumed to be highly disposed to support psychoanalytic thought in general, certainly not Reichian thought. It was Brinkman's fate to be the Council's leader during the early ebb tide of psychoanalytic influence in the training of ministers. The tide was against him. The Reichians were not yet outlawed by the Council, but they were soon to be. Their sun was setting. They were still functioning in Texas into the 1950s, but soon never to be heard from again. Even the memory of them is mostly erased.

Brinkman was succeeded in his leadership of the Council by his associate, Fred Kuether, who became the executive director on a part-time basis. Keither did not hesitate to exercise his administrative authority to discipline outliers in the community. In 1948, he removed the credentials of a Reichian supervisor, on somewhat vague grounds, but nevertheless sending a signal to all Reichians in the Council community.[20] This action was also a subtle message to sexual liberationists of any sort. Kuether resigned in 1954 after six years in the position. A replacement for Kuether could not be found at the salary level offered. A secretary, Emily Spickler, was hired as administrative assistant. She rose to the position of executive secretary and remained in the position until 1961. The irony here is that both the Council and the Institute seemed to be in administrative disarray, lacking in leadership as well as being at odds with each other, but they each continued to increase their numbers. It seems to have been a new age of prosperity for the clinical training movement, in spite of being bereft of strong leadership. Or was the prosperity in fact attributable to the absence of strong leadership?

At the same time there was a battle underway over the question of whether clinicians should be considered pastoral counselors and/or pastoral psychotherapists. Fred Kuether and Carroll Wise led the argument, following Boisen, that pastoral clinicians are *ipso facto* pastoral psychotherapists. But they did not have the critical mass to carry the day on that argument. Thus, in 1960, an entirely separate organization was formed, the American Association of Pastoral Counselors (AAPC). They chose the weaker label, 'counselors', rather than 'psychotherapists'. AAPC is still in existence, but in a state of decline. State licensure of pastoral counselors in several states has weakened them further. However, the very existence of the AAPC has weakened the Boisen movement as a whole by its implication that a rigorous course of additional advanced clinical training is a prerequisite for the work of pastoral psychotherapy.

Hiltner's attempt in 1944 to bring all parties to the table in the First National Conference on Clinical Pastoral Training was a harbinger of things to come, but it would be a quarter century in getting there. It was seven years later, in 1951, before its sequel, the Second National Conference, convened for the purpose of furthering Hiltner's initiative. At that meeting the so-called "Committee of Twelve" was created. The Committee consisted of representatives from each of the presumed stakeholders, the Council, the Institute, the Lutheran Advisory Council, and the Association of Seminary Professors in the Practical Fields. The Committee was assigned the task of creating standards that would unify all the disparate groups committed to clinical pastoral training, and to create one national organization. The stated objective was to create standards that could be embraced by all participants. They worked over the next 16 years before reaching an agreement on a proposal that could be expected to pass. We note that Joseph Fletcher, who was conducting clinical training under his own name in Cincinnati and Boston, was in attendance at the 1944 gathering. But he did not remain involved in efforts to create a single organization. He may have been wiser than all the rest.

Several forces were simultaneously at work in the wider clinical pastoral movement. There was a strong antipathy in the Council toward the Reichians in their midst. At the same time many in the Council wanted training to be something very close to psychotherapy, particularly for beginning trainees. All the while, the Institute leaders were attempting to quash psychotherapy of any sort and focus on a philosophy of education. But within the Institute, with Cabot dead, there was an insurgent interest in psychotherapy, an echo of Boisen, albeit psychotherapy à la Carl Jung. These conflicting tides of philosophical opinion represented what Chuck Hall later called an "unarticulated secret movement." Eventually history was going to demonstrate that psychotherapy of any sort would be trumped by a theory of education.

Nevertheless, leaders of both the Institute and the Council continued to seek rapprochement. In October 1949 the leaders of both organizations gathered again at Perkiomen Inn, in Schwenksville, Pennsylvania, seeking unification. It was almost a disaster and dampened any hope for unity. The Institute delegates viewed Council supervisors as rebellious, irresponsible, impulsive, and acting out. The Council viewed its adversaries in the Institute as rigid, compulsive, judgmental, and adept at using intellect to avoid feelings.[21]

That future could have been predicted from the makeup of that 1951 meeting of the Committee of Twelve. The seminary representatives strongly supported clinical training, but they leaned more favorably toward the more intellectual and academic approach of the Cabot tradition, which was embodied in the Institute. The Lutherans were primarily interested in preserving their own theological orthodoxy, and their representatives were divided, some certified by the Council and some by the Institute. Thus, the Boisen group, committed to a psychoanalytic perspective and also unnerved by the Reichians in their midst, was destined to lose its preeminence in the Committee and also to lose in any up or down vote. As movement toward union progressed, the clinicians of the Council implicitly gave away the authority to govern themselves.

Meanwhile, pastoral clinician outliers continued working independently as if nothing was happening on a national level. Boisen continued working in Chicago; Joseph Fletcher in Cincinnati and Boston. Wayne Oates and the Southern Baptist Association for Clinical Pastoral Education (SBACPE) were organizing in the southern states. They would eventually become a force to be reckoned with and demand a seat at the table.

In March 1957 the Committee of Twelve reconstituted itself as the Advisory Committee on Clinical Pastoral Education, the purpose of which was the same: to create a federation of all parties holding an investment in clinical pastoral training. Membership was enlarged to include regional representatives and representatives from the Association of Theological Schools, as well as the National Council of Churches. This further diluted the voices and votes of the Council representatives. At the next meeting, in 1959, the Advisory Committee was led to believe that the finalization of the federation was imminent. Ominously, the Advisory Committee declined to allow debate on any differences in philosophy of training, differences that were clearly represented by the Council on the one hand and the Institute on the other. The fact is that some of the new members of the Advisory Committee knew little or nothing about such philosophical differences. In 1960 a meeting was called that was billed as the time for final approval for a federation. At the last minute, both the Institute and Council voted against it. The motivation for the negative vote was an objection to the inclusion of an upstart denominational group who were requesting a seat at the table, the Southern Baptists (SBACPE). While the Lutheran members of the Association were individually certified by either the Council or the Institute, none of the Southern Baptists were certified by either of the two established organizations, the Council or the Institute. This gave the Southern Baptists the aura of outsiders, and of illegitimacy. Thus they were denied membership on the Advisory Committee and the movement toward federation was halted in its tracks.

The Southern Baptists were indeed an upstart group, formed in the 1950s, and they seemed to have been off the radar until the moment in 1960 when their request to be included on the Advisory Committee—and implicitly in the projected federation—was presented. The refusal to admit them brought about the defeat of the proposed federation itself. It would take another seven years of negotiations before the federation was ready for approval, and by then the Southern Baptists were solidly in—and dominant.

During all this bureaucratic wrangling, the entire clinical movement continued to prosper in its many warring subgroups. The Council grew from 17 training centers in 1947 to 43 a decade later. Its income tripled. The Institute, though smaller, was also prospering. But the Southern Baptists, beginning with only Wayne Oates in 1947, were growing at a faster rate than either. By the time the 1967 federation was accomplished, in the form of the Association for Clinical Pastoral Education (ACPE), the number of Southern Baptist supervisors was 80, representing the largest group and more than one-third of the total membership that formed the new federation. Most notably, and curiously, 20 of the 80 supervisors in the Southern Baptist group were not actually Southern Baptists by religion, but were from a variety of other denominations. The SBACPE was an ecumenical gang.

The sudden appearance of the Southern Baptists was phenomenal, like mushrooms after rain, sowing confusion among the older, established organizations, the Council and the Institute. The creators of this new organization were Wayne Oates, Richard (Dick) K. Young, John Price, and Myron Madden, each a liberal Southern Baptist, totally immersed not only in water but also in Sigmund Freud. Oates was the leader of these insurgents. More than a decade earlier, after Oates had completed two units of training, the second one with Boisen himself, he made application to the Council for certification as a Supervisor. The Council Executive, Fred Kuether, interviewed Oates (presumably alone) and denied him certification. Clearly, that was not going to be the correct decision going forward.

Fifteen months after his rejection by the Council, Oates became on his own authority the training supervisor for clinical programs in four hospitals in the South, two general and two psychiatric. Oates, Madden, and Young became the preeminent supervisors in the southern states for decades to come, for the rest of their lives. Madden occupied New Orleans; Young, Winston-Salem and North Carolina; and Oates, Louisville. They were a brilliant and dynamic threesome.

Oates, Madden, and Young attracted a great number of promising protégés and the SBACPE, for which Oates was the leader, certified them.

The four organizations coming together would then be five. The admission of the SBACPE added to the weight of the Council philosophy. The SBACPE was strongly Freudian. But Thornton believed this difference could be managed. His view was that the root of much of the conflict in the movement as a whole was in setting the shepherding and healing perspectives over against each other. Physicians and analysts only heal. Community organizers, and most religious leaders, only shepherd. Pastoral clinicians, in Thornton's view, should function both as shepherds and healers. Even the Freudians could accept that. That is what might have been.

When the federation was finally sealed in the fall of 1967, 256 supervisors were inducted into the newly formed Association for Clinical Pastoral Education (ACPE). Ninety were from the Council, 72 from the Institute, and the remaining 94 were from Oates' orbit. It was an astonishing accomplishment for a man who was denied certification by the Council in 1946 and was blocked from participating in planning the new federation in 1960. Once again, the stone that the builders rejected had become the chief cornerstone.

Thus the new Tower of Babel was completed in 1967. All clinical pastoral supervisors were now to speak the same language. Rejoicing and self-congratulations abounded, except for an unspecified number who did read the fine print, some of whom bolted.

Under the radar the language was the language of Cabot, not of Boisen. The chaplain was now cast as the physician's helpmeet. A large part of the attention was on the words of the prayers given by the chaplain, not the words of the patient. The importance of listening went into gradual eclipse. The question of the person and the psyche of the chaplain was put on the back burner or ignored. The psychoanalytic perspective was replaced by theories of education. Malcolm Knowles replaced the psychoanalytically oriented Rudolf Eckstein and Robert S. Wallerstein as principal theorist of clinical pastoral supervision. Freud went into eclipse. This massive shift in the philosophy of training did not occur instantly. It was gradual. But it was relentless. And it was a massive defeat for the Boisen approach to training. Fortunately he had died two years previously. To be sure, it took some years for the effects of this revolution to be felt at the grassroots. Most supervisors, whether formerly of the Council, the Institute, or from the Oates orbit, generally went on doing what they had always been doing. However, the effects were ultimately felt in all their fullness as the years passed.

In another 20 years, the ghosts of Boisen, Dunbar, Hiltner, Oates, and others would begin making their voices heard again in new incarnations. The principal form of that new creation was the College of Pastoral Supervision and Psychotherapy. Only Oates among the original key leaders was still living, and in hand-written letters to me he strongly approved. He died in 1999.

7.
WILHELM REICH: THE ORGONE AND PASTORAL CLINICIANS

Wilhelm Reich, born in 1897 of Jewish parents in Central Europe, was one of Freud's most brilliant and innovative protégés. He met Freud in 1919, a very young veteran of the Great War. Freud took an immediate liking to him and employed him to do administrative and therapeutic work at his clinic. He was something of a prodigy. He had taken an apartment at Bergasse 7, just doors from Freud's address at Bergasse 19. At age 22, and while still in university, Reich was authorized by Freud to analyze patients. There is little doubt that Reich was some kind of a whiz. Nor is there doubt, as was later found out, that his personal boundaries were close to nonexistent or that he was at least slightly mad. (But then, too, so was Boisen!)

The principal theme in Reich's life and work seemed to be the conviction that satisfactory sexual experience was the one and only basis of health and happiness. This extreme emphasis soon alienated Reich from Freud and from most of the rest of the psychoanalytic community.

Reich migrated around Europe in the decades between the wars, ultimately dodging the Nazis as well as many of his own former colleagues in the psychiatric community. Freud eventually considered him to be beyond redemption. In 1939 Reich was permitted to immigrate to the U.S. and was on a passenger ship to leave Norway just before the Nazi invasion. Columbia University psychiatrist, Theodore Wolf, assisted Reich in getting a visa and getting established in a teaching position in the U.S. This was during the time Wolf and Dunbar were divorcing. They had married in 1932. Dunbar's own thoughts and feelings about Reich are not currently known. But it is known that Dunbar hired the Council Supervisor Robert Brinkman, a Reichian himself, to succeed Seward Hiltner as executive secretary for the Council in 1938. Wolf actually mentored Brinkman in Reichian therapy.

Among other things, Reich invented what he called the Orgone Accumulator, commonly known as the "orgone box," a contraption about five feet in height, somewhat resembling a phone booth, in which one sat for purposes of restoring one's sexual energy. The first orgone box was built in 1940, in the U.S. Numerous literati made use of the orgone box, including Norman Mailer (who possessed three), J. D. Salinger, Saul Bellow, Sean Connolly, Paul Goodman, Alan Ginsberg, and other notables. The comedian Orson Bean wrote a book, *Me and the Orgone: The True Story of One Man's Sexual Awakening*, published in 1971, describing the therapeutic benefits of orgone therapy. Bean writes that he found Reichian therapy after 10 years of ineffective psychotherapy.

One professorial maven from Washington state was reported to have said he had no confidence in the efficacy of the orgone box, but that his wife sat in it four hours a day, and for that he was very appreciative.

In the 1950s, the Food and Drug Administration (FDA) got Reich in their gun sights and prosecuted him, describing his orgone box somewhat over-heatedly as "a fraud of the first magnitude." This resulted in a sentencing of Reich to two years in Lewisburg Federal Prison, in Pennsylvania. Six tons of Reich's books and papers were then burned in New York City's Gansevoort Incinerator on 25th Street, in 1956. That may have been the largest book burning in American history, just two decades after Adolf Hitler's book burning frenzy in Germany. One must wonder what ghosts Reich stirred in the psyches of those in power in the FDA.

In 1957, at age 60, just prior to his scheduled parole, Reich was found dead in his prison bed. His death was attributed to a coronary attack.

During Reich's European days, Freud wrote in a letter to Lou Andreas-Salome:[22]

> We have here a Dr. Reich, a worthy but impetuous young man, passionately devoted to his hobby-horse, who now salutes the genital orgasm as the antidote to every neurosis. Perhaps he might learn from your analysis of K. to feel some respect for the complicated nature of the psyche.

There is a lot that is not known about the relationship of Reich to the early pastoral clinicians of Boisen's clinical training movement. However, it is clear that a number of the supervisors in the 1940s and 1950s used Reich's theories and practices to one extent or another. The actual extent may be lost to history because of the negativity of the public response to Reich. I can testify that Reich's books were seen by me on the bookshelves of many supervisors in the 1960s. But I do not know of much that was written about him or how much he was actually used in clinical pastoral training. Probably not much, at least directly. Perhaps this question would make a Ph.D. research project for some energetic soul who could comb the archives of the clinical training organizations for Reichian fingerprints.

I have never stumbled yet on a comment on Reich by Boisen, though he certainly mentions other protégés of Freud, such as Pfister, Jung, and Adler. My assumption is that Reich's elevation of sexual agenda above all else would have been quite unacceptable to Boisen, especially since it was unacceptable even to Freud.

I have no record of how Dunbar assessed the theories of Reich, or what she thought of her husband's involvement with Reich. Her appointment of Brinkman to replace Hiltner in 1938, who had been tutored by her first husband in Reichian therapy, certainly suggests that she at least had no particular brief against Reich. On the other hand, they were divorcing during that period.

Part of the problem was that the details of personal sexual behavior and values were a particularly serious taboo in that era. Sexual matters were simply not discussed in public. Paul Tillich was highly promiscuous. Karl Barth lived under the same roof sexually with two women, his wife and his mistress, for most of his adult life. The sexual life of U.S. presidents were never a subject of public discussion. It was a different era from the one we presently live in.

As mentioned earlier (Chapter 5), Robert Brinkman was general secretary for the Council from 1938 until 1946, and a known Reichian. Even so, he seems to have had a sterling reputation, as testified to even by Ed Thornton as well as Institute leader, Richard Lehman, in an unpublished paper.

While Reichian theory was being dismissed in the eastern U.S., it continued to remain alive at least for a while in the Southwest, at least as late as the early 1960s. According to Council Supervisor Winton Gable, a personal friend of mine, Al Sherve, a Council supervisor, drove to meetings of the Council with an orgone box strapped to the roof of his car. A photo of that would be gold.

Perhaps the most candid account of Reich's influence on early supervisors can be found in an unpublished paper written by Gable and sent to George Buck. Gable was a Council supervisor from the 1950s, a Texan, an extremely thoughtful and kindly man who assumed significant leadership roles in the Council and subsequently in the early decades of the ACPE. In the early 1970s he was chair of the Southwest Region of the ACPE. He was consistently nonreactive, low-key and just, with a piquant, understated sense of humor, very much reminiscent in irony and verbal rhythm of the comedian Bob Newhart. Gable was a good friend of mine.

In a personal letter to me late in his life, Gable related his own brief encounter with Reichian therapy. Gable trained at Terrell State Hospital in Texas where Council Supervisor Walter Bell supervised him. Bell was a proponent of Reichian therapy. Gable says that the state hospital was relaxed about orgone treatment for patients. In that era of warehousing psychiatric patients, hospital administrators were happy for most any kind of patient support. Gable says he did not know whether Bell possessed an actual orgone box, but that he was aware that Bell offered Reichian therapy to hospital patients. As Gable describes it, the patients—male or female—were asked strip down to their underwear and lie on a couch. At some point, presumably in the context of conversation, Bell would physically and vigorously stimulate the patient to orgasm. Bell offered to train Gable in the method, even though the Council had by now officially disapproved of it. Gable declined, partly because of fear for his reputation in the Council, which he hoped would ultimately certify him. And he added also that two of his patients were young attractive women, and he feared he could not maintain a professional role in working with them in a Reichian modality. Finally Gable wrote me in a personal letter that if he had the same offer today to be trained in Reichian therapy he would readily accept. Had he accepted Bell's invitation, as he later believed, it would have saved him the necessity of other kinds of therapy later.

The encounter between Reich and the clinical pastoral movement seems mostly lost to history, alas. Perhaps in some attic somewhere or in some archives there is more data yet to be found.

8.
SPEAKING WITH ONE VOICE: THE CREATION OF THE ACPE

The merger of the four groups into the newly created federation, called the Association for Clinical Pastoral Education (ACPE), was not a peaceable transition. And the decision to merge was actually a close thing. It was not a decision based on consensus. A close majority ruled.

The merger was driven in part by the promise of a gift of $100,000 from W. Clement Stone, an offer conditioned on the creation of the merger itself. The offer was initiated by Arthur Tingue of the American Foundation of Religion and Psychiatry. Stone and Tingue scheduled a breakfast meeting with Chuck Hall, President of the Council, and John Billinsky, President of the Institute. Stone viewed clinical training as a promising discipline for addressing issues of spiritual and mental health, and was insistent that clinical supervisors work more closely together in one organization. Stone himself was a follower of Norman Vincent Peale's positive thinking approach to problems. Stone had personal links with Richard Nixon and also with the prosperity preacher, Robert Schuller. Stone was also a devotee of Carl Jung and had sent his son to be analyzed by Jung. Those clinical pastoral supervisors of that period, who were in the process of distancing themselves from Freud in favor of Jung, would likely have had an affinity with Stone.

In the 1967 meeting in Kansas City, which officially created the ACPE, Stone was presented with an award for his funding and for sponsoring the merger. He was invited to speak. Hall says that Stone seemed to "forget the nature" of clinical pastoral training in his "somewhat long address." Stone expounded on ideas of the power of positive thinking. After the address, Hall drove Stone to the airport. En route Stone said, "I don't know what was wrong. The audience was polite, but was not hearing my message." Though Stone must have arrived home close to midnight, the next morning a truck arrived at the ACPE meeting with a complimentary copy of Stone's book on the power of positive thinking for each member of the conference. Several years later he also made a matching grant in support of the *Journal of Pastoral Care*.[23]

Opposition to the merger was fierce and ongoing. It seems in retrospect that there was an urgency to unite this band of a mere couple of hundred professionals who hoped to change the world. At the same time there was a palpable sense that a merger would result in silencing some voices and put an end to the diversity that was dramatized in the ideological conflict between the Council and the Institute. The key leaders of both the Council and the Institute opposed the merger, as did a concerned minority. Those who felt indebted to Boisen and the Freudian tradition were the most troubled by the proposed merger. Their opposition was loud and persistent. Oral tradition holds that Chuck Hall called the question, using Roberts Rules of Order to quash further debate, and the motion to create the ACPE carried. Hall in his own book denies this, but he does assert that he strongly supported the merger and was happy to see the question called. John Billinsky, who once called Council Executive Fred Kuether's training "pseudo-therapy," called for a delay. He argued that Hall was rushing the decision. Billinsky was so offended at what he considered a rushed decision, and that Hall had somehow railroaded the merger through, that for years he refused to speak to Hall. Former Council Executive Fred Kuether also opposed the merger as a rush job.[24]

Apparently the judgment of the majority in the Council was that the differences in philosophy in the Council and the Institute could be resolved as time went on. The desire to be one community prevailed over the concern that in the merger one philosophy or the other would come to dominate the movement. In fact that fear was realized. Boisen was being sold out. Following the vote a number of supervisors walked, feeling that their philosophy had been betrayed. George Tolson, Nick Risted, and Len Cedarleaf were Californians who were a vocal part of the Boisenite protest.

The ACPE immediately formed itself into nine geographical subgroups, which it labeled "regions." Hall contended that by subgrouping the newly formed ACPE into nine regions, the organization as a whole would continue to nurture face-to-face relationships that he viewed as essential.[25] The subtext was that supervisors were traditionally suspicious of centralized power. None of the regions permitted their regional directors to work for the central office, for fear of national domination.[26] To support regional development, Hall called for $1000 grant to each of the regions.[27] To some extent Hall's vision was fulfilled. However, as the ACPE doubled in size, most regions became rather large, diluting the face-to-face, interpersonal dimension. Exactly 50 years later, in 2017, the ACPE officially abolished regions altogether in favor of a more centralized control, much to the chagrin of many of its members.

In spite of John Billinsky's uneasiness about what he saw as the precipitous creation of the ACPE, he would have been comforted had he been able to see the future. What, in fact, did occur in the merger was the gradual establishment of Cabot's philosophy as the orthodox position for clinical pastoral training. This was not done suddenly or dramatically but quietly and by attrition. And it enabled many of the Boisen followers to relax and let history run its course. The first signal of a Cabot takeover, however gradual, was the naming of education as the mission of the new organization. Boisen saw his project as training as opposed to education, following the medical model of post academic training. Trainees became students in the new organization. Seminars became classes. Lectures often took the place of case studies. And the verbatim, a narrow slice of a brief encounter, supplanted the case study, a wide view of the patient, as the focal point of training. The philosophical basis of training was shifted from psychoanalytic theory to educational theory, from Sigmund Freud to Malcolm Knowles. The new focus was on how trainees and patients learn rather than on the complexities of unconscious processes and how to engage patients and trainees therapeutically. Boisen's books soon fell out of print. There was less attention to the person and character of the supervisor and more attention now to the knowledge possessed by the supervisor.

As time passed Freud and psychoanalytic theory were referred to less and less. For those programs with any interest in psychology, Jung's was generally the psychology of choice. Perhaps the *coup de grâce* was the bold declaration in the ACPE documents, that "CPE was invented by Cabot and enlarged upon by Boisen." Thus, the creation of the ACPE was now explicitly a coup on behalf of Cabot and a diminishment of the importance and philosophy of Boisen.

The flawed presupposition that led to the creation of the ACPE was that there must be one controlling organization and one predominant ideology. It is a destructive principle, comparable to the claim that there must be one Christian church. Such a posture always means the suppression of many dissident voices. It is a recurring impulse. The old Council itself had taken a similar posture toward the Reichians in the 1940s and 1950s.

The enforcement of the new regimen came about gradually. Supervisors, being who they are, generally went on doing what they had been doing all through the decades to undermine and disenfranchise the Boisen tradition. And the fact of the matter was that Boisen's philosophy remained relatively alive and well in the ACPE during the first two decades. I personally served on the Regional and National Certification Committee from the mid-1970s until the late 1980s; I detected no obvious onslaught against the Boisen philosophy. Myron Madden and Wayne Oates were still active and vocal. George Buck, who was a strong Council supervisor, chaired the national ACPE Certification Committee for three years in the 1980s. The attrition of the Boisen perspective was certainly gradual, though in retrospect it was relentless.

The following chapters will explicate some of the lines of battle in the new ACPE. In addition to the dethroning of Boisen's psychoanalytic perspective and the enthronement of educational theory, I will elaborate on the gender conflict that dominated most of the agenda in the ACPE for the following half century. Many of the women came into the ACPE with a chip on their shoulders and a determination to even the score with men in one generation. It was an interesting time to be alive, but it was more interesting if one was of the female gender.

The various pastoral clinicians, who in 1967 were creating a new organization, could not have been aware of the significance of cultural developments that would do more to shape the character of the ACPE than any of these ideological differences. The Sexual Revolution was, in 1967, only a small cloud on the horizon. But it soon became a tectonic shift in the culture, forcing societal changes that few could have imagined. The clinical training movement was virtually an all-male community in 1967. Helen Flanders Dunbar, as Boisen's right hand at the beginning, had been the rare and notable exception to a leadership that was entirely male. In less than a generation, women largely would seize the reins of the movement. The character of these women varied from person to person, but the aggregate of feminine voices carried problematic negative overtones. There were recurring suggestions that it was payback for males who had suppressed them for so long. There was a tendency to see all males as authors of and supporters of an abusive patriarchal system, and therefore culpable.

Furthermore, most of the new women came into the clinical pastoral movement without any significant experience in congregational leadership. This was no fault of their own. Most congregations in that era were wary of female leadership and unwilling to accept a woman pastor. This lack of early formative pastoral experience in congregational leadership prior to undertaking the teaching of the next generation of pastors had a weakening effect on the training of the next generation, the perennial task of clinical supervisors. In 1967, a candidate could not be certified a supervisor absent "significant pastoral experience." Seven years of congregational pastoral leadership was generally considered minimum. Later, women were given a free pass on this issue—arguably just in light of the realities of congregational attitudes toward women—

but the free pass also shaped their philosophy of pastoral care in ways that limited them. As if this were not enough, a large percentage of the incoming women clinicians were homosexual, typical of one gender penetrating the discipline of the other, and this fact further complicated candid and open relationships between men and women. The following pages will elaborate on some of the evidence of this developing state of affairs—or should we say, this developing crisis.

9.
MY OWN ENTRY INTO THE CLINICAL PASTORAL WORLD

Into this maelstrom and completely unaware of the larger issues, I joined a Council program in July 1967, just as the Council as an organization was about to be disbanded and absorbed into the ACPE. I was oblivious to these organizational configurations and would not have fathomed the implications even if I were informed of them.

After seven years of experience as a parish minister I entered clinical pastoral training for the first time. It was the middle of a summer training unit at St. Luke's Episcopal Hospital, in Houston. The fact that the training group was already well underway, at about the halfway point, did not matter to Armen Jorjorian, the supervisor. He did things his way, as Frank Sinatra liked to say.

I had managed to avoid clinical training as a seminarian seven years earlier at the Presbyterian Theological Seminary in Richmond, Virginia (formerly Union Theological Seminary). I was serving two small rural Methodist churches in nearby Chesterfield County, and I appealed to Dean Lewis to exempt me from having to take clinical training. I argued that I was already working with people pastorally and clinically in my two churches. He readily agreed, which revealed how little he understood clinical training. I won the argument but lost the war. I was working for sure, and working with troubled people, but I had no clinical supervision. And if anyone needed clinical supervision, it was I.

When my seminarian friends who took the prescribed summer of training returned to seminary in September—several were trained by Pat Prest at the Medical College of Virginia—I immediately noticed that they were different. In conversations with them I noted a subtle change in their way of seeing things. They also had a slightly different way of relating to me. They were not at all hostile, just different. The difference in them somewhat unnerved me, though I was more intrigued than put off by it. I certainly took note, but I plodded on for another half dozen years and three failed pastorates before I decided, in desperation, to undertake clinical pastoral training myself. It was either that or leave the ministry. In retrospect, of course, I know what the difference was. They were in tune with their unconscious, and I wasn't.

In 1967 I sought an internship that would offer me clinical training, with a stipend. The differing philosophies of training were unknown to me at the time. I made my own assessment of programs by attempting to read the character of the supervisor himself.

I was accepted by Charles (Chuck) Hall at the Topeka State Hospital program and by Armen D. Jorjorian at St. Luke's Episcopal Hospital program in Houston. (Hall would become the first executive director of the ACPE in the following year.) By some happy accident, or through the mysterious workings of the unconscious, or perhaps Providence itself, two psychoanalytically oriented supervisors accepted me. I elected to train with Armen, undoubtedly because he clearly communicated his positive feelings toward me, that is, his own positive transference. He also offered me a higher stipend, $4,000 for the year, instead of the $3,500 offered by Hall. Armen was a stocky descendant of a family of Chicago's Armenian rug merchants. I had no real idea of what I was getting into. I did perceive that many, if not most, of the pastoral clinicians I had encountered seemed to know what they were doing and spoke with some personal authority.

After I arrived with family and belongings, and was fully in the process, I was required to pay some minimal fee for one thing or another. I presented Armen with a personal check. After looking at it, he asked how it was that my bank was located in Portsmouth, Virginia. I explained that my father and grandfather were bankers; it was their bank. I had a complimentary account there. After a pause Armen asked, "How old are you?" The long and short of this encounter was the suggestion that I was rather late in reflecting on my parental ties and my dependency issues. All of that gave me a start, of course. But I did contract immediately with a Houston bank and opened an account. Armen also insisted that I would not likely be successful if I failed to engage a personal psychotherapist. And I did that too, without much delay.

I decided very early in the training year that I should seek supervisory training. Armen supported me in that ambition, but on the condition that I first complete a year of internship. He also recommended that I seek another program for my second year of training. His view was that training for two years in one program would not be optimal. In retrospect I believe he was exactly correct. All supervision is different. It's all very personal and idiosyncratic. Exposure to a different perspective, even if the two are in general accord, is beneficial. In retrospect I now also see that Armen sent me away so that he could bring me back later as a junior member of his staff, something he could not easily have done had I done both my training years with him.

Clinical pastoral training is always focused on the dual agenda of learning how to be more appropriately therapeutic with others—patients, clients, parishioners—while at the same time coming to terms with oneself. Training is very much a parallel process, and sometimes one is caught up short with that awareness. I like to relate the very instructive vignette my friend and colleague, H. Mac Wallace, tells of himself. He captured simultaneously the spirit of both psychotherapy and clinical pastoral supervision. Mac brought a dream to his supervisory session one day, a dream that deeply puzzled him. In the dream he was raging against his father, saying to him, "Do not touch my wife!" Sharing the dream with his supervisor, after some reflection his supervisor asked, "Does that mean that you were thinking of touching his?"

For my second year of training I cast about for available residencies that carried stipends and found a program that I liked, Central State Hospital in Milledgeville, Georgia. (In spite of my family banking history, I had no financial reserves or external support.) The institution was far removed from St. Luke's Episcopal Hospital in Houston, though it was also a psychoanalytically oriented training program. Central State was more like a large warehouse for psychotic and otherwise disturbed humans, situated in a small rural town. Chappell Wilson became my primary supervisor, along with Don Cabaniss, Ron Wilkins, and several others. Wilson and Cabaniss had been certified originally by the Southern Baptist certifying group and had been under the hegemony of Wayne Oates and Myron Madden, persons immersed in psychoanalytic theory and practice. Cabaniss actually conducted seminars in psychoanalytic theory for the medical residents at the hospital who were preparing for their psychiatric board exams. He was the in-house expert on Freud. I was impressed that the administrator of the hospital, who was a psychiatrist, had contracted with a Baptist cleric to teach Freud to young physicians and budding psychiatrists. That fact disclosed a lot about the nature of the Boisenite wing of the clinical pastoral training movement in the 1960s. Jerry Jenkins and Zeke Delosier were also strong influences on me. After a year in Milledgeville and receiving credentials as an Acting Supervisor from a committee chaired by John Patton, who told the committee that he wished I were staying in Atlanta, I was on my way back to Houston to become a junior member of Jorjorian's staff. St. Luke's Hospital at the time may have been the largest training program in the country. A 500-bed hospital, it supported seven full-time chaplain supervisors and 50 trainees at various levels of training, from stipended residencies on the one hand to novice seminarian volunteers on the other.

In the fall of 1970 I was certified as a full supervisor in the ACPE. I had passed the bar. Chuck Hall, ACPE Executive Director, unexpectedly sat in on the Certification Team at the last minute for reasons not explained to me. He actually participated in the review, which as executive director was certainly his prerogative.

Perhaps I was already seen as a suspicious character. Or perhaps Jorjorian himself was being surveilled. Or both. The review was no walk in the park, but it was one of the most affirming events in my life.

10.
ARMEN JORJORIAN AND THE MURDER OF JOHN ROLLMAN

When I began my own clinical training in 1967 under Armen Jorjorian, the second-in-command in the Department of Pastoral Care was John Rollman, an acting supervisor under the Council and an Episcopal cleric. It was known that John was homosexual, but the matter was never openly discussed. Homosexuals in those days, just prior to the full bloom of the Sexual Revolution, were generally relegated to the proverbial closet. Rollman could not have held his job were the matter a subject of public discussion. When I was a trainee John and I had little interface. He never supervised me or conducted any seminars in which I was involved. Later, in 1969, when I joined the staff, John and I became good friends. Even then, the subject of his sexual orientation was never broached in conversation. John was, in most respects, extremely reserved. He kept his own counsel. But Jorjorian held him in high esteem and I appreciated his friendship.

At some point in those early years John, credentialed then as an acting supervisor, presented himself to the ACPE for full certification as a clinical pastoral supervisor. The gossip focused on his sexuality and whether the Certification Committee would turn him down because of his obvious though closeted sexual orientation. There were a couple of other supervisors in the ACPE known to be homosexual, but there was also an undercurrent of homophobia in at least parts of the clinical pastoral community, and it seemed to exacerbate after the creation of the ACPE. Sure enough, John's presentation of himself to be certified as a full supervisor was rejected, not explicitly because of his sexual orientation but on other grounds, which I do not recall. The grapevine held that the negative result was due to his homosexuality. With Armen's encouragement John appealed the decision, a rare thing to do in those days. I do not recall what the substance of the appeal was, or whether I even knew at the time. But the hidden agenda was certainly that he got no fair hearing because of his sexual orientation. I do recall that John told me that he went to a bar and ordered an Old Fashioned just before the committee hearing, to calm his nerves. He was certified on appeal.

The few reputed homosexuals that I knew of in ACPE remained very much in the closet except for one bold supervisor working at St. Luke's Hospital in New York City. In that city he did not feel he needed to be in hiding as regards his sexuality. The ACPE, like its predecessors, was, generally speaking, a liberal community in those days, but there were some subjects that were rarely discussed openly, sexual identity being one, and especially homosexuality. But the Sexual Revolution was at that time building up a head of steam, and the landscape would soon be altered.

In 1973, John was murdered in what appeared to be some kind of sexual encounter originating in a gay bar in Houston. It seems he went to the bar, contrived an assignation with a young man, a transvestite as it was reported, and left the club with him. Two men accosted them in the parking lot, forcibly locked John and his consort in the trunk of their car, drove to the banks of the Trinity River off Interstate 10 east, and killed John. He was forced to strip naked. Pleading for his life, as was reported by his consort, he was bludgeoned aside the head with a tire tool and left in a ditch. His "date" was brought to a hospital with minor injuries, and I had a phone conversation with him. He would not talk more than giving me the bare details of the killing. It happened on a Saturday night. I found John's prepared Sunday sermon on his kitchen table later, when I brought his parents from the airport to his home. The sermon's text was, "He shall be like a tree planted by waters...." The police apparently did no serious investigation, and it was said that the Episcopal Bishop "encouraged" the news media to downplay the "incident." I recall one conversation with the bishop on the matter. He asked me at one point, "Raymond, how are you using that word, 'transvestite?'" I had the devilish impulse to respond, "Just as the dictionary specifies, Bishop." But I decided that would not be good for my future in the Episcopal Church. John's murder was hushed up and never resolved—probably never even investigated by the police, even though John's consort almost certainly knew the identity of the killers. After all, John was a homosexual.

Armen Jorjorian was not in Houston when John was killed. He had left to become the Dean of Seabury-Western Theological Seminary in Chicago. He was pressured to leave Houston by the local Episcopal clergy and the bishop. The bishop forced him to close down completely his clinical training program. For Armen that was tantamount to being fired. After Armen left Houston, the clinical training program was reinstated, with a considerably smaller budget of course, and I was made Interim Director. Armen was too powerful a personal presence for the local clergy to tolerate. He intimidated them. The depth of his wisdom and his personal presence frightened them. I recall the bishop once said to me after Armen had left: "Armen would just look at me without saying anything." He made the bishop nervous. It was clear to me that Armen was hoping the bishop would recognize his own need for psychoanalytically based pastoral consultation. The bishop could have used it, but it was not to be.

I was the one who informed Armen in Chicago of John's murder. After some thoughtful reminiscing, Armen remarked, "It seems at least that John was getting well." Armen took John's willingness to go to a bar to seek out a homosexual partner to be a sign of his growing maturity and social courage, an indication that he had begun to come to better terms with his sexuality.

Abortion was illegal in Texas in the 1960s, as in most of the U.S. The family of an earlier congregation that I had served in Newport News, Virginia, phoned me in 1968 to ask me what they could do about their 16-year-old daughter who through a careless sexual act was pregnant. While I stewed over the matter, not knowing what to recommend, my assertive wife went to Armen Jorjorian on her own (let's say, behind my back) and asked him what we might do for them. Though she barely knew Armen, she had a better instinct than I did that Armen was both, as Yiddish puts it, a macher and a mensch. And yes, Armen was in contact with an underground network in Longview, where a licensed medical doctor was willing to do a safe and professional, though illegal, abortion. So my wife met the girl on arrival at Houston's Hobby Airport and escorted her on a puddle-jumper flight to Longview for her procedure. The pilot had a horn that he sounded from the cockpit to signal the plane's arrival at Longview airport. Armen clearly risked his job and public standing for a girl and family whom he did not know and never met. He could have been subjected to criminal penalties had anything gone wrong. Nor would Armen likely have found much support either from his fellow clergy or from his fellow pastoral clinicians of the ACPE. The old Council that Armen began with was being morphed into the more respectable community of the ACPE, where the 1995 Standards read:

> In all professional matters the ACPE member maintains practices that will serve the public and will advance his or her own profession.

And,

> The ACPE member abides by the professional practices and/or teaching standards of the state, the community, and the institution in which he or she is employed. If, for any reason, he or she is not free to practice or teach according to conscience, the member shall notify the employer and the ACPE through the Regional Director.

Times had changed. In the 1960s Armen Jorjorian risked his professional reputation in supporting homosexuals and a desperate, pregnant unmarried teenage girl who was known to him only as a friend of one of his trainees. Armen came of age in the old Council and he lived its spirit, the spirit of Anton Boisen. I do not believe he foresaw the barren years that were soon to come, as the spirit of "The Council," as it was called, was suppressed in the new amalgamation, the politically correct ACPE.

Armen died prematurely in 1973, at age 54, suffering from a congenital heart defect. Armen was a man of strong personal authority, and in that regard was an exemplar of the best of the Boisen tradition. He was also a man of liberated sexuality and in that regard he brought into my generation the best of the liberal values of the old Council.

11.
THE EMERGENCE OF WOMEN

In 1969, there were two women supervisors in the ACPE, Helen Terkelson, certified by the Institute, and Louise Long, certified by the Council. My path never crossed with either of them. Only in the late 1970s did women begin emerging as clinical supervisors. The reason for this paucity of women was that there was hardly a reservoir of women clergy from which to draw. During my two years of training, 1967–69, I do not recall that any women participated at any level, and my recollection is that this was the case universally. However the initial signs of the coming Sexual Revolution were all around us. The sexual mores were changing almost imperceptibly. There was ferment in the culture at large. It was evidenced on Broadway, and evidenced more particularly in the religious communities, particularly in the Catholic convents. One of the results of that ferment was that tens of thousands of Catholic nuns—in fact the majority of them in the U.S.—were beginning their exodus from their convents. And a lesser number of Catholic priests were leaving the priesthood. The Sexual Revolution was in part a clarion call to the celibate world that they were sacrificing too much, or sacrificing the wrong things. Many of the religious celibates, particularly the nuns, found their way directly into clinical training programs, as a sort of professional halfway house, where they could often receive a modest stipend while learning clinical pastoral skills. It was a natural stepping-stone into the secular world. Most of them seemed to be simultaneously undertaking both training for a new kind of pastoral work and also trying on their first real sexual experiences—or perhaps their first heterosexual experiences. Many candidly shared stories of their homosexual adventures in the convents. It was a very yeasty time. The entire clinical training movement was sexually invigorated in very public ways that certainly would have shocked and disturbed the sexually abstemious Boisen, who had died in 1965. It is just as well that he did not live to see the Sexual Revolution in full bloom. He would almost certainly have been dismayed by such liberated and open-faced sexuality. However, it was a creative time to be part of the clinical training movement.

The flood of former nuns entering clinical training, along with numbers of Protestant and Jewish women, soon radically altered the gender makeup of most training programs and ultimately the movement as a whole. From two women supervisors in 1969, the numbers increased to 114 supervisors 20 years later, representing about 20 percent of the number of active supervisors. Homosexual supervisors also came out of the closet. So the character of the small band of clinical pastoral supervisors, numbering about 500, excluding retirees, began to become more representative of the wider community, embracing all genders, sexual orientations, and religions. And in a mere handful of years clinical pastoral training morphed from an almost exclusively male Protestant enterprise into a mixed gender and interfaith enterprise. In retrospect, I do not recall any serious conversation among pastoral clinicians reflecting on the possible social and psychological impact on a community experiencing such a monumental transformation in such a short time. If my memory serves me, we all went into this upheaval blindly and unquestioningly, but certainly with a positive attitude initially and no sense of trauma. My colleagues seemed quite delighted with the change, as I was. After all, what could be more boring than working exclusively with Protestant heterosexual males? The influx of women, gays, Jews, and Catholics was stimulating and welcome. (The Eastern religions were to appear later.) But we were not savvy enough to reflect seriously on the potential implications, positive and negative, of such a radical change in the composition of the community. Had we been wiser we might have better prepared ourselves for trouble that should be expected when a community radically alters its makeup. The unconscious will always collect its debts. For a community that identified itself as profoundly clinical, the dearth of serious reflection on the radically changing religious and gender aspects of its membership was, in retrospect, passing strange. It was certainly a failure of self-reflection. And self-reflection is the alleged indelible mark of pastoral clinicians.

By about 1980 the good feelings around gender inclusiveness began to dissipate. Had there been an authentic prophet in our midst, he or she would have announced that a penalty would soon be exacted on males as a gender, signifying their responsibility as a gender for subordinating women for so long.

Male hostility toward women was not the problem; rather it was their unawareness of the predicament of women and a failure to identify. An illustration of this lack of awareness was the decision of the leadership to hold Certification Committee meetings at the Playboy Mansion in Chicago in the 1960s. When I heard of this venue, even as a trainee, I was somewhat taken aback. I was hardly a prude, but I recall feeling that the leadership was not minding the store, that the symbolism here was poor. Decking young women in Bunny costumes was not a road to empowerment. And the innuendo of a playboy was a model of boys with too much excess money. Astonishingly, even after women began flooding into clinical training, the Playboy Mansion continued to be used as a venue for meetings of pastoral clinicians. My friend Medicus Rentz met and passed his Certification Committee there in 1974. He still has his souvenirs from the Mansion. These committee members who established such meetings were not women haters, but they demonstrated a certain obliviousness to the feelings of women. My presumption is that this was the last of such Playboy Mansion meetings. The flood of women already entering the community would not have tolerated many more such meetings.

In the late 1970s a small band of the newly certified women supervisors began meeting as a separate group. They requested financial support from the ACPE to publish a newsletter specifically for women in clinical pastoral education. Their request was denied, correctly. The leadership's counteroffer was for them to publish a section in part of the established *ACPE News*. But the women raised their own money and published their own separate newsletter anyway. This was the beginning of a clearly gender-based subgroup with substantial boundaries and a hint of gender animosity. A major liability in this was that men generally did not see the newsletter, and they were the ones who ought to have seen it. The women's seminars were billed as "Women Supervising Women," signaling the women's dismissal of the value of male supervision. A gulf was developing between the genders at a time when the genders ought to have been openly meeting, talking, and even fighting. A significant number of the newly certified women turned openly aggressive and surly. In the face of this escalating hostility most of the men became increasingly passive. It seemed as if the women might be determined to exact some penalties on males for the generations, even eons, of subservience to males. The complaint itself had historical legitimacy. But to assume that centuries of gender abuse could be assuaged in one generation and the penalties be paid by one gender was in retrospect illusory. Contemporaneous males could not in reality be expected to pay the bill for the long and immemorial history of male domination and/or abuse.

The increasing male passivity was as if males were introjecting the women's charges and willingly carrying the guilt of generations before them. Obviously, this was not a strategy that was going to end well, but no one at the time seemed even to be aware of what was happening around them. I do not recall any thoughtful or reflective discussion taking place on the matter at the time. The angrier women became, the more passive men became. In my tentative engagement with ACPE leadership on the issue, the stock response I received was simply that things were going to be different from now on. Of course, that conclusion did not take much reflection or wisdom.

To blame women in general would gain nothing. The women had good grounds to be angry. They and their mothers before them had been mostly excluded from the profession from time immemorial. Furthermore, now that they were included they found male passivity at the helm. Passivity is worse than hostility. Thus there were now two reasons to be angry. That no leadership emerged that was potent enough to force an honest engagement of men and women on a level playing field, with a venting of the abuses on both sides, was an enormous lost opportunity. This was a community of theologically and psychologically informed professionals (allegedly), and they could not find a way to sit down and talk about the increasingly inflamed relations between men and women in their own midst.

The substantive loss in all this was that this professional community, originally founded on a commitment to understanding unconscious processes in individuals and groups, was now engaged in open gender warfare, and floundering, and unaware of what hit them. Unconscious forces were marching the community to war. No one took side bets on males coming out on top.

12.
THE GEORGE BUCK CASE

George Buck had been a clinical pastoral supervisor since the early 1960s, first as acting supervisor with the Council and then as a full supervisor with the ACPE, as that organization absorbed the Council in 1967. George was a close friend of mine. He was the typical training supervisor of the day, smoking, drinking, and with little regard for middle-class sexual mores. Over the years it was the alcohol that brought him down. His inordinate drinking was no secret to the community of pastoral supervisors, but through the decades he was never confronted. His employer, Austin State Psychiatric Hospital, ultimately moved against him. George was spending his workday afternoons in local bars drinking beer—lots of it. He lost his position at the hospital. A year later he was appointed to a United Methodist Church pastorate where he continued drinking. Before long the United Methodist Church's Board of Ministry summoned George for a hearing and confronted him with his drinking. George laughed off the query, adding that he drank only beer. For the time being denial protected him. At the same time, disciplinary action was proceeding against George, at a snail's pace, in the ACPE.

George's own United Methodist pastor, working outside the church's bureaucracy, then organized an alcohol intervention of the sort designed in the 1960s by Dr. Vernon Johnson. I was one of the six or so persons invited to this surprise confrontation, as were a couple of other long-time friends of George. His ex-wife, since deceased, and a couple Methodist clergy were a part of it. George's own pastor chaired the intervention, in 1984.

George, of course, was surprised by this meeting. His ex-wife lured him to the meeting by deception. He was taken aback to see me there, my having flown in from New York City. He of course denied that he was actually an alcoholic, repeating once again the claim that he drank only beer. He fought off the intervention for some time. Finally, George's own pastor reported that the bishop supported the intervention, that the bishop guaranteed George a pastoral position if he completed the treatment course successfully, and that the United Methodist Church would front the cost of the treatment until George was able to repay it. At that, George ended his resistance, and was on a plane to the Hazelden Foundation, in Minnesota, for treatment a day or so later. It was remarkable that a United Methodist pastor, supported by his bishop, would take initiative and act more compassionately and with more authority and clinical savvy than the ACPE itself, posing as a community of experts in pastoral care and counseling.

During the 30 days George was in treatment, he received a registered letter from the Judiciary Committee of the ACPE to the effect that his credentials as a certified clinical pastoral supervisor were rescinded. The Judiciary Committee had been duly informed during its meeting, held in San Francisco, that George was at that very time in treatment at Hazelden. George had earlier been notified by mail that he would be permitted to appear in person before the Judiciary Committee, at his own expense, if he elected to do so. He did not intend to attend, for money reasons as well as reasons of pride. The judgment against George, as he reported it, was couched in vague terms, of his "violating certain standards." The failure to specify what standard he had violated was contrary to the spirit of the Boisen movement. In fact, it is contrary to common law practices where persons are entitled to be informed of the substance of their alleged crimes. George's misuse of alcohol would, of course, have been reason enough to take action against him. In any case, George's credentials as a clinical pastoral supervisor in the ACPE were rescinded, a message he received while in treatment.

The ACPE Southwest Regional newsletter then published an announcement stating that George was about to be indicted by the Texas Attorney General, presumably for unspecified misconduct in his role as Director of Chaplains at Austin State Hospital. No such indictment was ever put forward. This was further despicable treatment by the ACPE of a man who, whatever his flaws, had given much leadership to the community for several decades, and was currently in treatment for alcoholism.

Thus, after years of service as a certified Clinical Pastoral Supervisor, first in the Council and then in the ACPE, and having assumed a number of significant leadership positions, including a three-year term as national Certification Chair, George was summarily removed from the ACPE community and his credentials were taken from him without even so much as a face-to-face encounter. It seemed clear to me that the ACPE professional community had undergone a radical change, and had assumed a vindictive spirit. It had traditionally, in its earlier iterations, been a strong face-to-face professional community with considerable flexibility and open-mindedness, and with a mark of the countercultural.

Subsequent to his treatment at Hazelden, and several years later, George was certified by the CPSP and functioned honorably for another quarter century, ultimately retiring from University of Arkansas Medical Center in 2015.

My perspective on this episode was that the radical feminists in ACPE, with the support of passive males, were driving the case against George. That is not to say that he was innocent. It is to say that the insurgent female leaders identified him on the grapevine as an abuser of women and this undocumented innuendo propelled the overly zealous efforts to undo him on the legitimate charge of alcoholism. As was usual at that time, males who might have come to George's defense were silent, compliant, and along for the ride. There is no known evidence of any specific charge filed against George for sexual abuse of a woman. Whether there should have been is a matter of speculation. Popular opinions do not rise to the level of substantive charges.

By the 1980s a large contingent of women had been certified as clinical supervisors. In this influx a disproportionate number of these women were of the radical feminist persuasion, many of them militant lesbians, and it was apparent that they had long-standing personal agendas with males in general, and especially with heterosexual males who possessed personal authority. This energy was directed particularly at males who were, as we used to say, sexually liberated. This was perhaps understandable in that these women were entering a profession that had heretofore been almost universally reserved for males. It was apparent that these women intended radically to change the ethos of the ACPE and of society generally. They were particularly prepared to challenge any taint of male chauvinism. Such chauvinism, of course, ought to be challenged. However, in at least some instances there were ill-considered conclusions about what constituted male chauvinism. George Buck was a ready-made symbol of the kind of male the radical women sought to punish. The fact that he was hard drinking, heavy smoking, and sexually uninhibited fed that image. Whether or not he was in fact abusive to women, such evidence was never presented for scrutiny. My impression was that George had a preference for female over male trainees, but that in itself is not a crime. The absence of official grievances, save one unspecified one, does not make him innocent of abusing women, but it is worthy of note. My contention is that this assault on George Buck was one of the first shots in a gender struggle in ACPE designed to disempower strong heterosexual males. And to a large extent it succeeded.

A real irony of this skirmish was that the women who sought to punish George for his sexually liberated behavior were the same women who themselves were demonstrating their own sexually liberated behavior. One of the principal leaders of feminist coalition at the time was an active United Methodist minister who lived openly with her lesbian lover. Such a sexual arrangement was a violation of the United Methodist Church's Discipline at the time, and had she been publicly charged she would likely have lost her ministerial credentials. Thus, some of the most vicious women in their dealings with strong heterosexual males were themselves proponents of a liberated sexuality; but it was to be a liberation only for homosexual women. The times were crazy making.

13.
JOAN E. HEMENWAY

Joan Hemenway was a strong player in the ACPE community in the last quarter of the 20th century. She was arguably the most powerful woman in the community during that era.

I first met her when she appeared before the ACPE national Certification Committee sometime in the late 1970s, as I recall. She was one of the first women in that large group of women who was presenting herself for certification, and she appeared before my subcommittee. I was impressed with her presentation of herself and her personal authority. This all-male certification subcommittee unanimously approved her.

I met her next in 1983 when I moved to New York City. Joan was at that time the administrator for an agency that later became the HealthCare Chaplaincy. She was also by then a powerful person in the Eastern Region of ACPE, just having been elected regional director. In an effort to connect with key persons in the region, I asked her to join me for lunch soon after my arrival. She agreed and we had our lunch, but she was rather reserved, bordering on cool with me. I never did figure out which of my many attributes might have been seen by her as objectionable. It was likely something she had heard about my role in the Southwest Region where I had held some leadership positions. I remained in the Eastern Region for five years, until 1988, and never felt very welcome by the leadership that surrounded Joan. I was hardly a novice or a wallflower. I expressed interest in undertaking some leadership role in the region, but was never authorized to do so, nor was I brought informally into the region's inner circle.

In my final year in New York I was called by the Nominating Committee chair, who asked if I would agree to serve as one of three members of the History Committee. I agreed. I was also aware that in terms of power and status, the History Committee was the very bottom of the bucket. But everyone has to start somewhere. When I arrived at the Regional Meeting where the elections were to take place, I noticed that my name did not appear on the list of nominees for the History Committee or any other office. So I managed to work five years in the Eastern Region without holding any leadership position in spite of my experience and my offers to serve. I was fully aware that I was being sent a message, and my suspicion was that the message came from the recently enfranchised women, Joan being their leader. I had taken a bullet for the men in an early skirmish in the war of the sexes.

My isolation in the Eastern Region was at least part of what fueled my motivation to stir up some trouble with my newsletter, *The ACPE Underground Report,* which I composed during my last months in New York, mailed out only a month prior to my departure for Virginia and the Mid-Atlantic Region. On arrival in Virginia, in February, I was assigned a position on the Regional Certification Committee immediately and was put to work on the Certification Committee that was meeting the very next month. Serendipitously, I was assigned a roommate, Perry Miller, whom I had never met, nor even heard of, but who ultimately became my closest friend and colleague. Later on Perry and Robert Claytor joined me as founders of CPSP. At dinner the first night of that meeting in March, Perry asked the group of diners, "Who's the guy that sent out that underground newsletter recently?" He obviously had paid no attention to my name appearing in the text as the "angel." As could be expected, Perry got some laughs for that.

In the first issue of that newsletter I caustically mocked the Eastern Region leadership as a group, and in particular, their manner of mutually congratulating each other publicly at regional meetings. This may have been revenge, of course, but the criticism was well founded and well deserved.

In a subsequent annual national meeting of the ACPE, a year or two after the start of my newsletter, I was mixing with a crowd on the first evening and came face-to-face with Joan. Before I could utter even a greeting, she physically lunged at me as if to do me harm. Fortunately for me, her friend John Swift (a big guy) was standing next to her and he physically restrained her. She could have done me some damage. Joan was a big, strong woman. And she was not happy to see me, to put it tamely. The gossip on her was that she arrived home from work one day in New York City to find a young man ransacking her apartment. She overpowered him, corralled him, and sat on him until the police arrived to take him away. The story is entirely credible. I am certain she could have easily whipped me, probably with one arm.

Eight years later, in 1996, Joan published a book entitled *Inside the Circle: A Historical and Practical Inquiry Concerning Process Groups in Clinical Pastoral Education.* It was the thesis for her D.Min. degree, a study of group process, Tavistock, in the clinical training tradition. She analyzed a hundred educational theory papers written for certification committees in the ACPE between 1988 and 1992. Her objective was to track theories of group supervision, as contrasted with individual supervision and case study seminars. Forty of the papers made no mention of group theory at all. Of the 60 that did, 19 referred to Yalom's individual therapeutic approach, 18 touted communication skills, 10 referred to Tavistock theory, and seven used family systems theory. Clearly there was no coherent or mutually agreed upon theory informing the group supervision aspect of clinical pastoral training in the ACPE.

Next, Joan acquired agreements from five female and 14 male supervisors who agreed to forward her a number of videotapes of their group sessions. As in the written papers the theoretical basis of these groups as illustrated in the recordings was all over the map. She categorized them in four types: 1. The group as education; 2. The group as individual therapy in a group context; 3. The group as supervisor-centered, in which the supervisor is presenting his/her own perspective, teaching, preaching, or self-disclosing; and 4. The group focused on unconscious material in the group itself with the supervisor commenting on here and now dynamics. The last of the four is the type of group that Joan regarded as appropriate to the clinical training context. The first three types Joan considered inappropriate. Her conclusion, though she is less than explicit in stating it, was that clinical supervisors generally do not know what they are doing when they conduct groups in the context of clinical training.

Joan proposed a remedy for such confusion—namely, that supervisors make use of the Tavistock approach to groups that originated with the late Wilfred Bion, the English psychoanalyst who came into his own in the middle of the 20th century. Bion's position was that unconscious processes take place not only in the individual but also within groups. Furthermore, Bion and his followers theorized that certain patterns of unconscious behavior, such as pairing, were endemic to group life and that examining such behaviors was both educational and therapeutic. Thus both the conscious and unconscious interactions among group members can be interesting and enlightening. Joan went so far as to bring Tavistockian consultants to meet with the Eastern Region. But she never ultimately attracted much interest from her peers in the ACPE.

I wrote a laudatory review of Joan's book, which was published in *The Journal of Religion and Health*.[28] She responded to me with a letter of appreciation, and we exchanged letters with suggestions that we should get together. For whatever reason neither of us broke the ice further, which was a great loss, and one that I very much regret. Unfortunately, Joan developed a progressive debilitating brain disease not too many years later and died much too young. Clearly she was a strong, bright woman with impressive leadership qualities. Her book remains a classic in the literature of the clinical pastoral movement even though there is little evidence that pastoral clinicians take it seriously. In fact, it may well be the most important book written by a clinical pastoral supervisor in her generation.

The irony here is that I, too, was promoting the use of Tavistock theory and practice within the CPSP, and had been since its beginning in 1990. Every national meeting of CPSP and every regional clinical seminar had featured a Tavistock demonstration seminar, in part as a way of introducing the Tavistock approach to the membership. I was introduced to Tavistock group work in 1975 and took consultant training with Margaret Rioch and Arthur Coleman for one long weekend in San Francisco in the late 1970s. Joan and I shared a deep appreciation for Bion's contribution to group work. The two of us were mostly alone in that appreciation. It was something that might have brought us together, alas. And together we might have been a blessing to the ACPE community.

14.
THE ACPE UNDERGROUND REPORT

In the 1980s, as I was participating in the national Certification Committee of the ACPE, I was beginning to make sense of the history of the clinical pastoral movement. I could see clearly that it had drifted far from its origins in Anton Boisen. Of course many others saw this long before I did. A decade earlier Robert Powell had attempted to call the ACPE back to its roots in Boisen's genius. He was the keynote speaker for ACPE's 1975 Annual Meeting celebrating the 50th year of the Boisen movement. He noted in his address that in this celebration the name of its founder, Anton Boisen, was nowhere to be found on the program. But no one seemed to be listening to Powell. Or perhaps they were listening and objected to the suggestion that the movement owed its existence to Boisen. Since Powell was never invited back to an ACPE event, the latter would seem to be the case. Even though he was pointedly ignored, Powell continued to function on his own authority as the preeminent historian of the clinical pastoral movement, and remains so today. He is without peer in this self-assumed role.

I could see as the years followed one another that my own pointed questions were getting under the skin of some of the leadership. In one sense I expected it, as the cost of raising questions in any context. In another sense it hurt me because I felt like the community of supervisors was my new church, so to speak, and yet I was being increasingly marginalized.

I attended the annual conference of the ACPE in Philadelphia in the fall of 1987. I generally avoided as much as possible the endlessly long lectures, one after another that constituted such meetings. It seemed poor pedagogy to me. So, as I was wandering around the hotel prior to lunch, I walked into a large room that was set up for the noontime meal. Duane Parker, the executive director, was at the far end of the large room speaking to someone, and he pointed over to me, and yelled, "There's trouble!" I knew that Parker was in part being affectionate. We had a cordial relationship, but I also knew that he did not like some of my several questions about the direction of our professional community. So his comment stung. I left the banquet hall and walked aimlessly into a lecture in progress, then winding down. Parker Palmer was speaking. It seemed to me that through the years Palmer spoke at every other ACPE meeting, as if no one else had anything to say, so I was not particularly receptive to Palmer. But just as I sat down, Palmer said, "If you can't get out of something, then get into it." Those words were like a message from the cosmic powers. I decided at that instant that I would be just what Duane Parker said I was, "Trouble." I went home and immediately began writing. I envisioned a private newsletter in which I would raise questions that no one seemed to want to hear. "Trouble" would be my new moniker.

Two prominent issues were at stake in my view. One was the abandonment of the philosophy of Anton Boisen, rooted as it was in psychoanalytic theory. Now this was fully 13 years after Robert Powell had wondered why Boisen's name did not appear on ACPE's 50th-anniversary celebration of the inauguration of clinical pastoral training. The other issue I intended to raise was the escalating pogrom against males as males, a fruit of the sexual counterrevolution. I intended to raise other issues as well. I vetted the first draft of my broadsheet with a half dozen trusted colleagues, each of whom gave me a thumbs up. I came to the realization, however, that no one had much of a taste for engaging this fight themselves, though I was certainly encouraged by many to take it on personally. I mailed out the first issue on January 1, 1988. I sent copies to about 500 names of clinical pastoral supervisors on the ACPE mailing list. I gave the newsletter the title: *The ACPE Underground Report*. I began naming what I saw as abuse, improprieties, lack of vision, and philosophical confusion within the ACPE.

In the initial issue, I did not identify myself as the author or publisher, but I did identify myself in the text as the angel (a deliberate provocation) who had financed the newsletter, which was of course true. No one else was identified by name because there was no one else involved. I was the writer, typist, publisher, financier, and errand boy. The alleged author was a fictitious invention with the contrived name, Boshenyetu Gospodyna Milyicertsova, which is Russian for 'No More Mr. Nice Guy.' I identified the author as a Russian, but apparently no one knew enough Russian to pick up the meaning of the name. "The Committee of Thirteen," which I alleged was supporting the newsletter, was pure fiction. There was no such committee. It was a playful allusion to the Committee of Twelve from the 1950s. I got so many requests for "the Thirteen" to step forward and identify themselves that in later issues I labeled them "The Cowardly Committee of Thirteen." Of course, in a real sense it was true. There were many people, far more than 13, who applauded what I was doing but did not want personal exposure. A few years later I established a real advisory committee of various members who did agree to have their names on the masthead. These were people who actually advised me. Along the way a couple of them resigned over one shocking issue or another that had gone to print without their consultation. However, the advisory committee remained a collection of reputable ACPE members through the years.

In the ACPE community there was an immediate and enthusiastic response, not from the majority, but from a noisy minority of several hundred. Many people sent subscription money and letters to the editor. I was suddenly notorious in the small, 900-member ACPE community, almost half of which were retirees. Overnight, I had acquired many friends and even more enemies. As could be expected, most of the women were de facto enemies. But in the course of a year, I had well over a hundred paid subscribers to my newsletter, as well as a greater number of freeloaders.

After three years, in 1991, I dropped the ACPE part of the name of the newsletter and continued simply as *The Underground Report*. Then, in 1993, I changed the name altogether to *Contra Mundum,* a phrase lifted from Athanasius of Alexandria, a not very admirable fourth-century Christian patriarch. He declared that he "stood against all the accepted opinions of the world." I certainly concurred with him on that posture, though I am sure that he and I hardly would have been in agreement on any specific issue in his world or mine. I finally published 106 issues over a 17-year period, until 2005. By then the Internet was making hard copy newsletters via the postal service seem archaic, and too costly as well.

The Underground Report was probably the smartest venture I undertook in my professional life. At the time, however, it seemed merely a way to vent my profound frustration with my role in life and my profession. Furthermore, it was the only recourse I had for simply protesting to whomever might choose to listen. As it turned out, many did listen, to my great satisfaction. And of course many did not.

15.
THE DEMONIZATION OF THE WHITE MALE

In the early 1980s, the ACPE grapevine reported that one of its certified male clinical pastoral supervisors had been charged by a woman, a former trainee, with sexual misconduct, and that his credentials had been lifted. As a consequence, he was dismissed from his chaplaincy position, was now unemployable in any similar position, and was reported to be working in a nursing home as a service chaplain. Though I knew the man only slightly from various organizational meetings, I phoned him and he willingly spoke with me. He was quite demoralized and I was sympathetic.

The story he told me was that he himself was married, and that he had been involved in an extramarital sexual relationship that continued for about five years with an unmarried woman who had previously been a trainee of his. He made it a point to say that the affair did not begin during the training relationship with her, but began after she left the program. He also reported that he had decided unilaterally to break off the affair and that his lover, in anger, had filed with the ACPE an ethical complaint against him. He shared with me the name of the woman who had filed the complaint, and she was someone I also knew slightly through professional meetings. I offered my sympathy and shared with him my view, based on what he had told me, that he had been dealt with unjustly. I encouraged him to keep in touch with me, and suggested to him—and I wish I hadn't assumed such a Pollyanna posture—that time has a way of healing most everything. Not surprisingly, I never heard from him again.

Shortly thereafter I discovered that the woman who had made the complaint had entered supervisory training herself with a distant colleague of mine. Some time after that I discovered that the woman herself was certified as clinical pastoral supervisor by the ACPE. And shortly thereafter she was elevated to high prominence as a key national officer in the ACPE itself.

The message to the clinical pastoral community was clear in this instance. In any kind of sexual liaison, if it is determined to have been an irregular relationship, the male will likely be punished and the female will likely be considered an innocent victim. That message was delivered across the clinical pastoral community in multiple ways, this episode being one early instance of it.

This vendetta against males as males was not really surprising. But what was surprising was that a community like the clinical pastoral community, psychoanalytically informed, allegedly, and committed to the highest religious values of justice and love, could support and even promote such a vicious campaign against males as males, as illustrated by the action against this one particular man. Occurrences such as this one motivated me to begin thinking of ways to protect myself in the years ahead. I could see that the slightest infraction on my part was going to be the end of my career. And because I had published a number of papers on the changing sexual mores, I knew that I had made myself a desirable target. I also noted that only males were charged with sexual boundary violations, never females.

And then came the 1990 annual meeting of the ACPE. It featured as keynote speaker an African-American psychologist, Dr. Edwin J. Nichols, who was assigned to address the community on problems of the relationship between the black and white cultures. His thesis was that minorities and women both were systematically discriminated against in the most insidious ways. He focused his particular attention on the sins and defects of the white male. He argued that the white male seems to need a more effective socialization. By innuendo he seemed to promote a sort of devil theory of the white male, who he argued needed to be retrained. I was astonished that the many white males in the gathering seemed to delight in the proposition that they were the source of what we know as gender and racial abuse. Nichols went on to attribute the then current Savings and Loan scandals to the fact that there were not enough women or minorities occupying seats on the boards of these guilty corporations.

Nichols' logic was not always easy to follow. For example, he attempted to disabuse the audience of the notion that males were physically stronger than females. "If you are so strong," he said, addressing himself to the males present, "try pushing a football through an orifice of your choice." The assemblage roared with laughter. I suppose his point was that the travail of childbirth demonstrates that women are stronger than men. But that did not persuade me. In general, males are bigger and physically stronger than females, even if they do not do childbirth. But so what? And what does that have to do with racial and gender abuse? And if females are actually stronger physically, why should they complain so much about physical abuse? They could fight back.

Next, Nichols went on to attack the late racist senator of North Carolina, Jesse Helms, which was fine with me. His point was to counter Helm's assertion that white people are losing jobs because of affirmative action programs. The whites, said Nichols, were only losing jobs that did not belong to them in the first place. In other words, where blacks are 50 percent of the population, they are owed 50 percent of the available jobs. Nichols' argument would have been less convoluted if he had simply contended that African-Americans were usually passed over in North Carolina, unjustly, when a white person was available for the same job.

Next, Nichols attacked the popular notion that ghetto mothers are having babies just so they can collect ADC (Aid for Dependent Children) payments. To prove his point he asked the audience: "How many of you have had a baby in order to receive ADC money? Please raise your hand." Not a single hand went up. "Interesting," said Nichols. "If it's not something done by women here, why should we think it is done by others?" he asked. Neither I nor anyone else bothered to speak up and say, "Maybe if one of us here were dirt poor, with no income at all, we too might have a baby or two or three in order to provide at least enough income in the form of public aid to survive. Isn't that to be expected from any oppressed group trapped in poverty?"

We learned from Nichols that women in black Africa are not subject to the same demeaning exploitation that women experience in this perverse white male culture. Well, maybe. No specific data was presented to support this dubious claim. Apparently Nichols had not been informed about the scourge of female circumcision in black Africa.

This was followed by Nichols' assurance that Eisenhower's mother was black, a fact covered up by the press. And also that King George III's queen was black, a fact also hidden from the public. But does anyone care?

At one point Nichols asked all the women present to stand up. Then, peering over the assembly he announced, "There are too many women here!" At that, many of the women sat back down. "Now you see how self-effacing women are," he added. "I said there were too many, and half sat down."

I found Nichols' pedantic superiority and silly gamesmanship off-putting, to say the least. At one point he asked the audience, "Now what day of the week follows Monday?" After the audience voiced the correct answer, Nichols replied, "Yes, Tuesday." He was attempting to make a point, but I lost what it might have been.

Astonishingly, Nichols seemed to have had the audience eating out of his hand, as they say. He had a long record of popularity in the world of pastoral clinicians, having previously spoken at the ACPE's Mid-Atlantic Regional meeting, the Southeast Regional meeting, and the Racial Ethnic Minority Conference. He was clearly on a roll with the ACPE. What his pronouncements had to do with clinical pastoral training was anyone's guess.

The ACPE paid Nichols $1500 for his speech of about an hour at that 1990 meeting. I suppose it was the organization's attempt to address racism and sexism in its midst. More likely than not, Nichols' presence actually fostered an escalation of racism and sexism.

A Communion Service was also held at that annual meeting. In light of the significant number of non-Christians in attendance, I thought it poor taste—even imperialistic—to conduct a Christian-style worship service. But the organizers did manage to de-Christianize most everything in the service except the label. Instead of the traditional Christian bread and wine for the Eucharist, they substituted orange juice; and instead of the usual Christian invocation of the body and blood of Jesus, the participants, in a posture of raw narcissism, were asked to raise their orange juice glasses and toast, "To us!" And they did. The high-minded Christian religious symbols of sacrificial love for the sake of the whole human community, though of course rarely demonstrated in deed, were replaced by a declaration of crass narcissism. I presume they were simply being honest. Honesty is also a virtue, I suppose.

In those years one heard radical feminists frequently employing the slogan "good old boy network" in reference to the clinical pastoral community. This was an effort to call attention to male privilege and abuses by the gender-based power structure. Undoubtedly there was some truth in the charge. A virtually all-male organization is bound to have some element of the good old boy network even as it moves toward a multi-gendered community. People are still people. And women had been blocked historically from significant and authoritative work in virtually every religious organization in the Western world. The Sexual Revolution itself endowed women with substantive equality. The clinical pastoral movement generally opened itself fully to women as professionals, and rapidly so. But it did not take long before a radical feminist network replaced the good old boys with the good old girls. And they proceeded to behave very much like the good old boys, if not worse. By 1990, the women were very much in control of the ACPE. But rather than using their newfound respectability and power to form a more equitable and just community, they used their power generally to engage in payback.

The fact that the ACPE community morphed from an essentially all-male community in 1970 to a community led mostly by females in less than 20 years should have been seen as a mark of progressivism and resiliency in the community as a whole. Males relinquished power in order to make way for females. The men should have been applauded for acceding to a more just and equitable community structure that was no longer dominated by males. Instead of applause they became objects of escalating contempt. Perhaps they were viewed by the women as cowards avoiding a fight rather than as progressives supporting a more equitable future. Undoubtedly there was some of each in the males.

16.
THE SEX SURVEY

In one of the early issues of my newsletter I decided to tackle the question of the views of clinical pastoral supervisors on matters of sexual behavior, specifically sexual relationships between supervisors and their trainees, and former trainees. Among clinical pastoral supervisors in the ACPE, there was considerable sotto voce conversation about sexual matters. And it was a poorly kept secret that a great many supervisors were known to have had sexual contact with trainees. Some had married their trainees. Some had had one or more sexual liaisons with trainees. And certain supervisors had established reputations (undocumented) for having rather large sexual appetites. But there was virtually no candid or serious conversation on the subject. It was seemingly a taboo to discuss the matter. It was the proverbial case of the emperor's new clothes. I decided to bring the discussions out in the open.

With the rise in numbers of women supervisors, this question became even more relevant and more sensitive. And with an inordinate number of the newly certified women supervisors being lesbian, the issue of sexual behavior became fraught with danger as well as energy. It is very curious to me, in retrospect, that there was never any public discussion of any ethical complaints against women clinical supervisors crossing sexual boundaries, only men. I heard of not a single woman being charged with sexual boundary violations, and yet it was apparent that in some instances such boundaries were being crossed. Some women supervisors were clearly becoming sexually involved with their female trainees, just as some men were. But in all such cases a discussion of the subject remained taboo. An open discussion was called for.

Thus, on September 1, 1988, ACPE *Underground Report #4*, I contrived a "Sexual Ethics Survey" to be sent by the ACPE-UR to 500 of the 900 listed supervisors, active and retired, on the ACPE mailing list. I limited myself to 500 simply because I did not want to purchase more stamps. A total of 164 responded, representing 24% of those who were sent the survey. This percentage of responses was comparable to a similar sexual survey done at the same time by the *American Journal of Psychiatry* which had a 26% return. Thus, we were in appropriate range of the kind of returns we could expect.

The survey contained 20 statements describing a potentially compromising position. Respondents were asked to give each statement one of the four following characterizations:

A) Morally reprehensible
B) Inadvisable or questionable
C) Morally unobjectionable
D) Don't know/impossible to determine

Listed below are the twenty vignettes with the percentage of the respondents who judged the action to be morally reprehensible. (The full survey is available in the archives, on request.)

1. A supervisor becomes genital sexually involved with a student in the course of a clinical pastoral training unit.
87% Morally reprehensible

2. Two supervisors, male and female, are married to other persons, allegedly in "open" or permissive marriages, meet at a regional meeting and become lovers.
42% Morally reprehensible

3. A male homosexual supervisor is attracted to a male student. Sexual identity issues are discussed in supervision, and the supervisor makes known his feelings. The student likewise feels very affectionate toward the supervisor and furthermore is ambivalent about his own sexual identity. In the course of the unit no physical gratification occurs except for a handshake. After the unit is over—the next day, in fact—the supervisor invites the student to a social event in hopes of developing an intimate relationship with him.
43% Morally reprehensible

4. A male supervisor who is looking for a wife becomes enamored of a female student. He decides that she is the woman he is looking for and that transference/countertransference issues have been satisfactorily examined. In the midst of the training unit he proposed marriage and she accepts. Because of their engagement, the student is reassigned to another supervisor for the remainder of the unit.
18% Morally reprehensible

5. A single homosexual female supervisor has a divorced female student who is ambivalent about her sexuality. The student is attracted to the supervisor and curious about her own potential for homosexuality. She even expresses her willingness to experiment. Near the end of the unit the supervisor invites the student to dinner at her apartment after which they drift into genital play. The next day in individual session they explore their respective reactions and reflections. No further sexual contact transpires between the two.
71% Morally reprehensible

6. A female student at the post-evaluation individual session at the end of a year's internship talks of her appreciation and affection for the supervisor because of what she has learned during the year. The student notices as he has on other occasions that the supervisor is sexually aroused as she talks. Unexpectedly and assertively she approaches the supervisor physically, unzips his fly, and performs fellatio on him. The supervisor accepts the deed after an immediate but mild protest. Afterwards she talks about how she simply wanted to do something especially nice for him and did not want it to go any further. Nothing further transpired between the two.
70% Morally reprehensible

7. A national officer attending a regional meeting encounters a single female supervisor-in-training at the meeting and, in a sexual liaison, spends the night with her. It turns out to be a one-night stand and no further intimacy occurs between the two.
62% Morally reprehensible

8. Two supervisors, a male and a female, each married to other persons meet at various professional meetings, and, over the course of two years, have an increasingly passionate affair, all the while deceiving their spouses.
81% Morally reprehensible

9. Another supervisor becomes privy to the relationship (in #8) and coincidentally is acquainted with one of the spouses, decides the affair is none of her business, and requires no action on her part.
16% morally reprehensible

10. A female supervisor and a male student, both single, acknowledge their mutual attraction for each other during a unit. Except for a cautious hug at the end of a supervisory hour, the relationship is kept free from personal gratification. At the end of the unit they agree to commence a personal relationship.
9% Morally reprehensible

11. A single male supervisor and a single female student are mutually attracted to each other during a summer unit. For several reasons, neither is interested in an on-going relationship in this instance. At the end of the unit, following a final Friday party, the two of them have a brief genital sexual encounter.
45% Morally reprehensible

12. A male supervisor cohabits with his female lover in violation of the stated moral discipline of his denomination.
32% Morally reprehensible

13. An experienced, mature, heterosexual female supervisor develops a close and affectionate relationship over the course of a year with a young male student who is sexually inexperienced and rather uncertain of his sexual identity. At the end of the intern year, motivated mostly by the student's need for experience, the supervisor invites him to her apartment for dinner and later to her bed.
69% Morally reprehensible

14. A homosexual woman supervisor lives with her lover in violation of the stated moral discipline of her denomination.
29% Morally reprehensible

15. A single male supervisor is known to date and have sexual liaisons with single women in violation of the stated moral discipline of his denomination.
36% Morally reprehensible

16. An experienced older single male supervisor meets an advanced clinical training student from another center at a regional meeting, and the two of them commence a serious dating relationship.
4% Morally reprehensible

17. A supervisor is made aware that a pair of his students have become genitally sexually involved. One is a male whose Protestant denomination prohibits non-marital sex and the other is a female in a Roman Catholic celibate order. The supervisor concludes that their sexual liaison is not a matter on which he can make a moral judgment. He concludes that, since the liaison has not adversely affected their work or training, no administrative action is allied for.
15% Morally reprehensible

18. A supervisor is apprised that a female student is dating a medical student and obviously sexually involved with him. The institutional administrator complains to the supervisor that this relationship is damaging the image of the chaplains' department. The supervisor notifies the student that she must terminate her sexual relationship or be terminated from the program.
27% Morally reprehensible

19. A female supervisor in a religious order requiring celibacy makes clear her personal dissent from the celibacy rule and also has a discreet but long-standing genital sexual relationship with a man.
24% Morally reprehensible

20. At a November convention, a supervisor unexpectedly meets a student who had graduated from the supervisor's program the previous May. They begin a dating relationship.
5% Morally reprehensible

The survey deliberately focused on third-party behavior. No question was asked about the specific personal behavior of persons participating in the survey. The reason for casting the survey that way was that the ACPE community was rather small. I could decipher the identity of some of the respondents by looking at the zip code on their mail. Typically there was not more than one supervisor living in a particular zip code. I figured that the respondents would be aware of that risk of exposure as well.

The survey results also suggested that while clinical supervisors were quite liberal, they were generally not comfortable with those who mixed ongoing supervision with sexual play. And it was also apparent that the respondents were generally more tolerant of female sexual behavior, as well as homosexual behavior when it might seem to be a boundary violation, than of similar male heterosexual behavior. That comports with other more circumstantial evidence in the same period. Heterosexual men were held to a more rigorous standard and more readily seen as culpable in those grey areas.

Many letters arrived commenting on the survey results. Some were published. The large majority of those who bothered to write were very supportive. Some were critical. A very few were highly critical or hostile. But of course I presumed that those most hostile simply did not bother to write at all.

The following letter, unrelated to the survey, but commenting on the newsletter itself, came from Carl K. Towley:

> What are we complaining about? The wailing and bemoaning of the sad estate of ACPE is what we deserve. The denizens of Cabot packaged and promoted the incremental losses, and we approved, yea, thundered our affirmation.
>
> The problem is not the potential political power of clinical members, neither the Certificates of Deposit or the condominiums, but our unwillingness to provide thoughtful alternatives and push for their adoption.
>
> The goal of education is being swamped in the morass of 'doing it by numbers.' For an organization that theoretically celebrates individuality, we are producing machines...Enclosed is my check. Wouldn't want to miss an issue.

17.
CIGARETTES, WHISKEY, WOMEN, AND POKER

On November 1, 1989, I published ACPE-UR #10, entitled "Supervisors and Whiskey and Wild, Wild Women," playing on the country-western song of similar title. Sections of that piece are excerpted below. I was highlighting the public reputation of clinical pastoral supervisors as a group. Obviously, not every supervisor fit neatly into this pigeonhole. The first executive director of the new ACPE, Charles E. Hall, certainly did not. He was for the most part a very straight arrow indeed, but not entirely. Charles, or "Chuck" as he was known, wrote late in life his memoirs entitled, *Head and Heart: The Story of the Clinical Pastoral Movement*. He recounted his own certification committee review in 1953, under the Council, as he presented himself for certification as a clinical pastoral supervisor. His account is quite candid:[29]

> It took place in an upper room at a retreat center on Lake Geneva, Wisconsin, a few minutes before midnight. This was one of the first years that the committee required written work from the candidate. It did not seem as if the committee members had read my material. Fred Kuether asked one question about my personal psychotherapy. My training supervisor, Thomas Klink, was asked about my work. After hearing from Klink, one committee member said, 'Klink thinks he's a good supervisor. I move we certify him.' It was unanimous and I was handed the open bottle of spirits (bourbon) from which they had been drinking. Offering me a drink was the symbol that I was accepted as one of them. This experience of sharing 'the cup,' as strange as it may sound to an outsider, was like a 'Holy Communion' for me. It was a sacred symbol of acceptance.

As a Methodist minister, Chuck was of course abrogating one of the principal ethical rules of his church at the time, imbibing alcohol. This was a symbolic act of rebellion against Protestant ethics in general, and it was characteristic of the entire clinical pastoral movement.

Though Chuck does not say so, his scheduled meeting with that Certification Committee was certainly not midnight. It is likely to have been something like 8:00 pm, or perhaps even 4:00 pm. The community of clinical pastoral supervisors that made up the Council was a small, freewheeling group. Even 15 years later when I appeared before such committees, they were typically quite casual and swashbuckling, and rarely on schedule—and similarly meeting late into the night. Sometimes, committee members would get into heated, extended verbal arguments among themselves and delay the hearings. And organizational politics was never far below the surface. If all that sounds chaotic, it was; but it was also creative, quite human, and on some level refreshing. These were professional clergy struggling with their profession, often disillusioned and wondering if they should be clergy at all. They had found something life giving in this connection to Anton Boisen and Sigmund Freud. But while they were followers of Boisen, he was not leading. In addition to that, he was a sometime psychotic, which never plays well in the newspapers.

One of the obvious manifestations of the personal struggle that these supervisors had with their calling is that they typically drank a great deal of liquor, sometimes even during committee meetings, as Chuck reported. Virtually all of them smoked, so that committee rooms were literally smoke-filled rooms. They played poker way late into the night for high stakes at many meetings. And they were known for what is now perversely labeled "womanizing."

In a rare instance of naming this behavior in writing, Walter Carlson charged in the Lutheran journal *Dialogue*[30] that CPE supervisors were not quite cut from the same cloth as other ministers. He was correct. They were making a profound theological statement—namely, that alcohol, gambling, sex, and tobacco were not the root of all evil, as was traditionally proclaimed by modern American Protestantism, even if the misuse of the same did create terrible personal and social problems. There did not seem, however, to be much traction for an open discussion of these issues. Furthermore, these upstart clergy were proclaiming that a competent pastor must learn at the feet of Sigmund Freud and be able to access basic psychoanalytic theory. And that was not fit news for the newspapers either, especially since Freud was known to insist that children were sexual beings.

Thus it was as if pastoral clinicians needed some public badge that would communicate their radicalism to society and the wider religious community, but to do so obliquely. A certain rough edge, a wildness signifying their radicalism, was intentionally stamped on supervisors from the very beginning. Or rather they stamped it on themselves. They needed such a branding as part of a declaration of their radicalism.

We must remember that it was a Methodist bishop named James Cannon, Jr., who had led the national campaign for Prohibition, a campaign that in 1920 succeeded in making the consumption of alcoholic beverages illegal. It remained the law of the land until 1933, overturned with the election of Franklin Roosevelt. *The Baltimore Sun* columnist and social critic, H. L. Mencken, wrote of Bishop Cannon in 1934: "Congress was his troop of Boy Scouts, and Presidents trembled whenever his name was mentioned.... But since that time there has been a violent revolution, and his whole world is in collapse." Mencken was correct. Prohibition was over. But the identification of Protestantism with Prohibition did not soon disappear. The followers of Boisen were, of course, no followers of Bishop Cannon. In fact, they were contemptuous of Cannon as well as many of the other major ethical principles of Protestantism. The early band of pastoral clinicians were misfits within their own religious communities.

As an aside, I was a teetotaling Methodist seminarian in 1956 who took his first year of seminary at the University of St. Andrews, in Scotland, and a second year at Mansfield College, Oxford. I had done my four years of college in the U.S., during which time I pledged to the Lambda Chi fraternity. I resigned from fraternity life after barely a year because of the emphasis on drinking. But I did not find such attention to alcohol among British Protestants. And I was quite taken aback when the dining hall waiter at Mansfield College took beer orders for lunch.

The flouting of American Protestantism's central behavioral codes by Boisen's followers was, in my view, a mere provocation, largely symbolic, like flag waving. I assumed it to have been a gesture signaling the pastoral clinicians' intention to reconstruct the basic moral assumptions of Protestantism.

Alcohol eventually lost its luster as a cornerstone symbol of the new dissident pastoral clinicians. Too many supervisors became alcoholics. But in other respects the rebellion against bourgeois and Protestant respectability continued. Poker games, with sizable amounts of money at stake, continued late into the night at most meetings. And tainted sexual activity among supervisors continued as a symbol of dissent against middle-class respectability. It is noteworthy that none of this rebellious activity on the part of pastoral clinicians was discussed openly. It was simply acted out. One had to listen as if to speakeasies.

It was only in the 1980s that smoking began to be prohibited in closed rooms, much to my relief. (I am a rare person in that I never smoked a cigarette in my life. Surrounded by cigarette smoke as a child, this was my form of rebellion.) The impetus for this radical change in public behavior was not specifically religious. It had become apparent in the culture at large that the use of tobacco carried serious health risks. I recall disrupting a Certification Review Committee meeting in that era because my good friend George Buck, the chairman, insisted on smoking in spite of an agreement in the clinical pastoral community that smoking would not be allowed in closed rooms. I won the argument, but almost lost a friend. And with the arrival of the Sexual Revolution the scandal of non-marital sex was minimized. However the subsequent sexual counterrevolution driven by the radical feminists reinstated penalties against sexual acting out by heterosexual males but only, as it seemed, for heterosexual males.

Today, these early badges of honor in the early clinical pastoral movement are outdated as instruments of protest. Alcohol and gambling are no longer illegal but au courant. Tobacco is in disgrace as a significant health risk. And the Sexual Revolution has knocked lifelong, monogamous, heterosexual marriage off its moral pedestal. However, Anton Boisen has also suffered a degrading. He spawned a religiously based psychotherapeutic mission that has been largely eclipsed, and alas, largely forgotten. While his legacy is being recovered in the CPSP community, that community is a minority of those who are now presenting themselves to the public as pastoral clinicians.

18.
DIALOGUE 88:
DEBACLE IN MINNEAPOLIS

On Sunday, October 30, 1988, all the major organizations in the U.S. that identified as clinical and pastoral were invited to gather in Minneapolis for what was billed as "Dialogue 88." CPSP did not yet exist. The ACPE *Underground Report* was ten months old and had published four issues. In retrospect, Dialogue 88 might well have been called "A Failure to Dialogue in 88." On the first day of the meeting, gossip was circulating to the effect that a member of the meeting had been mugged on the street between the hotel and the Convention Center. Sunday and Monday came and went, and the rumors continued. No one seemed to know anything about the incident except that a member of the meeting had been injured somewhere on the street.

On Tuesday morning the vice chair finally announced publicly that the Rev. Eugene Schwartzenberger had been mugged near the hotel and was in serious condition. Conference participants were advised to take taxis from hotels to the Convention Center or to walk in groups for safety and to remove their telltale name tag while on the street. Conferees were also advised not to investigate the matter and that they "should stick to what they do best—praying." Instructing many hundreds of persons not to investigate a matter but to resort to prayer is, from my perspective, like throwing Br'er Rabbit into the briar patch. Thus I decided to investigate. I did not find out much initially.

On Wednesday, it was announced that Schwartzenberger had died. No additional details were provided. Those who persisted with questions were directed to believe what they might read in the newspapers, upending that bit of axiomatic advice proffered by

President Harry Truman. And, of course, nothing at all had thus far appeared in the newspapers. The leadership of Dialogue 88 remained otherwise mute.

Then the Thursday edition of the local Star-Tribune reported that a visiting priest had died from injuries sustained in a local adult bookstore. Local television followed with a corroborating story. The first reports stated that he had fallen down a set of stairs in the bookstore. Later reports quoted the store manager as saying he had fallen after having been downstairs to watch adult videos in the private booths, as if to say he had fallen up the stairs rather than down. I phoned the city editor who graciously provided me with the address of the bookstore, which had not been previously made public. I went to investigate.

What I found was a store very close to the Convention Center billed as an Adult Entertainment Center. It consisted of a street level shop about 30 by 50 feet in size. A clerk was stationed behind a counter at the entrance. At his side was a closed circuit video system with several cameras for store surveillance. Sexually explicit books, videos, and paraphernalia were displayed in quantity, and essentially nothing else. At the far end of the store from the entrance was a staircase leading to a basement room. In the basement were several private, closed rooms for watching films. A sign was posted stating, "Only one person per booth except where indicated." Of course, nothing else was "indicated." When I was present the clientele were exclusively male. The way the clientele presented themselves and circulated left me with the impression that this store also served as a rendezvous spot for cruising gay males.

I queried the store clerk about the death, and he revealed to me that he was present at the time of the incident, that he had heard a commotion in the basement, and went to investigate. He found the victim at the bottom of the stairs. At the time of the incident there were several other persons in various viewing booths, he said. No one admitted to witnessing anything, he added. The clientele, he revealed, were mostly stray males. Then he turned away, signaling that he did not intend to answer any further questions from me.

The coroner reported that the victim died from a blow to the head, and ruled that foul play was not involved. The victim's valuables were not taken. The victim's brother told the press that his brother must have been in the bookstore to help someone. He had taken a leave from the priesthood at one point awhile back. Then he added that his brother had sexual-identity problems, and that there was a lack of a support system for such persons.

We will likely never know whether Schwartzenberger actually died from a fall down the stairs or from a sexual assignation turned violent. Either version of the event is plausible. He may also have been in the store to help someone, as the family suggested, or he may have been there for a sexual adventure. It seems most unlikely anyone will ever know what actually happened.

What is of more interest is the manner in which the clinical pastoral community, 1900 strong from a variety of religious organizations, responded to the event. Had Schwartzenberger been hit by a vehicle in the street and killed, we can imagine there would have been candor about the tragedy and openly expressed grief over his death, and some memorialization of the loss of his life. But because he died under sexually tainted circumstances, the entire body of pastoral clinicians, and particularly its leaders, was rendered utterly mute. This was a grim commentary on the capacity of pastoral clinicians to engage tragic human issues pertaining to off-the-beaten-path sexuality. The entire pastoral care and counseling community gathered in one place was made tongue-tied by the suggestion that irregular sex may have been connected to Schwarzenberger's death. The leadership of the Chamber of Commerce would likely have been able to respond more pastorally to the death of Eugene Schwartzenberger than this gathering of hundreds of the alleged top leaders of the clinical pastoral movement in the United States. A community that is unable openly to discuss matters of sexuality is an effete community that will not likely be productive in any sense. That the leadership of the movement considered the membership incompetent to cope with what was likely a sexually tainted killing of one of its own is testimony to the incompetence and sexual panic of the leadership itself.

A slot in the schedule of workshops during Dialogue 88 was billed as an evaluation session for the ACPE *Underground Report,* at my request. I hoped to receive some feedback on the effect of my newsletter in the community. About 30 persons attended, and the discussion was rational and useful. I chaired the meeting. A number of criticisms were voiced. Some criticized the anonymity, which was a bit humorous since I was it. No one else had been directly involved, and I had openly named myself in the first issue. Anonymity did not exist. No one seemed to catch the drift. Others objected to what they considered personal assaults on individuals, which was a fair enough criticism. I had felt that complaints or criticisms that sidestepped identification of individuals were too easily ignored. Vague inaccuracies were also alluded to. And indeed, there were some, but none of major importance. The Sex Survey was called "unprofessional." A charge of "too many typos" was made, which was certainly deserved, since I had not yet acquired the services of a proofreader. Of the 30 persons present, only one seemed to object in principle to what the newsletter was attempting to do, that is, to raise critical issues in the life of the ACPE.

A woman supervisor present, Cathy Bickerton, made the most astute and pointed criticism. She wondered if the newsletter might be motivated by anger among males, seeing the passing of the good old days when clinical pastoral training was the exclusive domain of a few "good old boys." Her question was a timely and appropriate one, slightly out of focus, but nevertheless pointing in the right direction. I personally was never aware of any regret among male members of the ACPE about women coming into the profession or into leadership. In fact, my impression was that men generally were delighted and greatly welcomed the women, and were pleased finally to be part of a truly multi-gendered community. I was on ACPE Certification Committees that certified many of the incoming women. There was not even a hint of male misgivings, as far as I was aware, about the large influx of women coming into supervisory ranks. I believe that Bickerton's question came out of the women's own projections, living as we all do in a male-dominated culture. She and many other women, I believe, simply expected to be resented and/or abused by males. Human communication being what it is, if one expects a certain kind of treatment, these expectations are often satisfied willy-nilly. In other words, the gender war was in part the result of women's projections. In fact, the community of pastoral clinicians was, as far as I could tell, well disposed to embrace women and to include them in the profession. Personally I preferred working with women, but I preferred women who seemed to enjoy men, and such women seemed increasingly scarce.

Bickerton was correct that some of the males were becoming alarmed, but that was only later when it began to be clear that many of the newly certified women were seemingly bent on making males compensate them for generations of patriarchy. Thus the witch-hunt began, searching for abusive males and allegedly finding them everywhere. And many of the women were determined to make unilateral judgments on what constituted gender or sexual abuse. In response to the witch-hunt, some of the males began to take action. One of those action responses was the *ACPE Underground Report*.

We must also note that the reacting males were far from a majority. Most males were quite passive in response to this gender conflict and passive as well in relation to the ACPE-UR. Barely 20 percent of ACPE supervisors subscribed to the newsletter. It must also be said that clinical pastoral training was never held in the possession of "a few good old boys." That is simply a politically motivated slur. Boisen's principal colleague and co-worker from the beginning was a radical progressive woman, Helen Flanders Dunbar. Without her, there would likely have been no substantive clinical pastoral movement.

The source of the gender problem was that the mission of Boisen and Dunbar involved training ministers, and that meant training almost exclusively men. There were no women ministers to speak of in any of the principal Protestant denominations until the 1960s. But I do not believe there was any substantive resentment among men about women entering chaplaincy. Quite the contrary.

The other source of female anger was more subtle and more substantive. It was, I believe, a response to male passivity in the face of the changing culture, and therefore eminently appropriate. I sensed that males—even clinicians—rarely talked straight to women in the same manner they spoke to each other. I believe this was motivated by fear of women. But it is a fear that some women learned to provoke. This would represent a kind of covert chauvinism that leads to resentment. It is not that males generally long for the alleged good old days (that never were), but rather that they don't know very well how to relate appropriately to assertive females. Nor do female clinicians know how to relate to male clinicians. In my view both genders have failed each other and now have some hard work ahead of them. Then when one adds to the mix an intense anger toward males in general among some homosexual women, you have a tinderbox ready for some serious burning.

On the day prior to Dialogue 88 there was scheduled what was billed as a "Women's Gathering." It began with a group march through the hotel lobby bearing feminist posters. As the marchers paraded by, a couple of the male observers joined in the march in solidarity with the women. (There were many committee meetings taking place in the days prior to Dialogue 88.) At the entrance to the meeting hall, to which the marchers were headed, female bouncers guarded the door to prevent entry by males. One of the male intruders who had spontaneously joined the march, a veteran of civil rights marches, bullied his way into the meeting, ignoring the bouncers. One of the women called out, "Let's go get Duane Parker (ACPE executive director)." When he could not be found, the women called Marriott security. They declined to act and referred the women to the police. The police arrived and, after questioning the women on the nature of the meeting and the intrusion, responded that recent legislation in Minnesota made it a criminal offense to refuse a person admission to a meeting solely on the basis of gender. The delicious irony here is that a civil rights law written to protect women from arbitrary exclusion was now being used to protect men proposing to attend a meeting that was designed to exclude men. Returning to the meeting hall empty handed, a bouncer then approached the intruding male and pled with him to leave voluntarily. He replied, "You and I have marched together for civil rights and for peace, and I don't understand why I'm not welcome to support women."

"We need to be away from men. The leaders are outside crying. You've upset them," the bouncer replied. The man stayed put. He was supported in his resolve by several women sitting near him.

After some initial speeches, two American Indian women came forward for what was billed as a "Peace Pipe Ceremony." But the women brought no pipe. Rather, they announced that since there were menstruating women present in the assembly, they would not be permitted to pass the peace pipe. They offered a prayer instead.

The male intruder left at noon and did not return for the afternoon session. One of the women who attended the afternoon session reported that the "menstruating women" story was a ruse, and that the peace pipe ceremony was cancelled because of the presence of the male. The covert message: "No peace with males!"

A number of males had actually registered in advance for the Women's Gathering, but in each case, allegedly, the registration was returned with a note indicating that males were not welcome. Since some names are sexually ambiguous, one wonders how the organizers distinguished with confidence male and female. And what about the cross-gender folks, and those of ambiguous gender? One also wonders how a "male only" meeting prior to Dialogue 88 would have been received by the women. Or better still, how about a gathering of white males only?

The Women's Gathering was philosophically bankrupt from its inception. Karl Barth wrote in the 1930s that religious gatherings should never separate into single gender groups. Pastoral clinicians caucusing into subgroups of particular gender, racial, or national identities poison the larger community. The Women's Gathering, in excluding men, actually subverted the dialogue of Dialogue 88. This malaise among the women was not a little ironic in that these same women, only a few years past, had been admitted into a profession that had excluded women for virtually all of human history. They should have been celebrating. Instead, they were declaring war on the same men who opened the doors of a previously predominantly male community to them.

Strangely enough, a psychologist was hired at Dialogue 88 to design the small breakout groups for the conference. The meeting itself was populated with a great number of trained clinical pastoral supervisors and pastoral psychotherapists, some with long experience in working with a variety of large and small groups. This demonstrated a lack of confidence in the wisdom of senior clinicians residing in their own midst and was an additional sign of failure in the clinical pastoral community at large.

A special closing event was held at Dialogue 88, a liturgical performance staged in a nearby Lutheran Church, featuring music and modern dance. I no longer recall the name that was assigned to it, but I do have a vivid memory of the performance. I personally entitled it "The Dance of the Quivering Poles." Four barefoot young women, dressed in long white gowns with red sashes, undoubtedly trained in ballet, paraded up the aisle bearing very long, flexible poles with multi-colored streamers attached at the top. These nubile ladies danced around the nave, up and down the aisles, making the poles sway and vibrate, and the streamers fly, all this accompanied by recorded music. They would occasionally stop, hold the poles tightly between their thighs and shake them vigorously, making the poles vibrate and the streamers fly high in the air. At the end, the lead maiden went to the dais, put down her pole, lay on her back and raised her legs up in the air. It was a nicely done work of performance art. Needless to add, the shaking and vibrating of these poles by those nubile creatures, accompanied by music, was quite inspirational.

I wrote a piece in *Contra Mundum* both praising the performance and wondering, provocatively, if the audience of pastoral clinicians had any notion of its apparent sexual innuendo. I did not hear a word afterward suggesting that anyone else had the same thoughts that I did. However, this being a gathering of pastoral clinicians, it must be assumed that others had similar associations. Certainly this piece of performance art, with its positive sexual innuendo, was a fitting close to a conference that began with the death—and likely murder—of a sexually troubled Catholic priest.

This experience also brought to mind an ancient Greek philosopher—which one I no longer remember—who on the streets of Athens during a celebration of the feast of Dionysus, commented to a colleague that the parading of those huge phallic representations would have been considered obscene were they not religious.

19.
THE DICTIONARY OF PASTORAL CARE AND COUNSELING

In 1990, a monumental publication appeared in the clinical pastoral world, *Dictionary of Pastoral Care and Counseling,* the fruition of a decade of toil. Rodney J. Hunter, a friend of mine, was editor. There were half dozen well-known and well-respected associate editors, one of whom was also my friend, John Patton. Five hundred and seventy-nine contributors received five cents a word for their twelve hundred contributed articles. Some of the contributions are brilliant. Many of the leading figures in pastoral care and counseling are among the contributors. Studying the 1990 Edition of *The Dictionary* now is somewhat comparable to an archeological dig. One can determine the nature of the debate and the nature of the distortions during the decade of the 1980s when *The Dictionary's* contributions were written.

As might be expected in such a monumental undertaking, there were notable quirks, or flaws—even howlers—in the collection. One quirk was that contributors from Emory University and Fuller Theological Seminary were dominant. Since the editor was teaching at Emory, that is understandable. The high profile given to Fuller Seminary, however, was a puzzle in that Fuller has a history being associated with fundamentalism. While fully ten percent of the contributors were from Pasadena, mostly at Fuller, only two percent of the published contributions were from scholars at Princeton, Harvard, Yale, and University of Chicago combined.

What was also striking about the makeup of the contributors is that, while about half of the contributors were practitioners, that is, pastoral clinicians as opposed to academicians, only a small percentage of the contributors were clinical pastoral supervisors. That discrepancy can be understood by the fact that by 1980, when *The Dictionary* was first being put together, clinical pastoral supervisors had developed something of a reputation of being unwilling or unable to write. My view is that clinical pastoral supervisors as a group went into a kind of eclipse subsequent to the merger of all the organizations into one, the ACPE, in 1967.

Subsequent to the federation or merger in 1967, pastoral clinicians increasingly took up the role of servants to the status quo and helpmeets to physicians, adding a prayer here and there to buttress the work of the authentic healers. The tradition of Cabot was in the process of edging out the tradition of Boisen. The emergence of the College of Pastoral Supervision and Psychotherapy (CPSP) in 1990, the year *The Dictionary* was published, attempted to reverse this trend, and began to do so with modest, gradual success. But the ACPE maintained its preeminence in the field and led to the dumbing down of the clinicians, which continues into the present. Thus the decade of the 1980s did not offer *The Dictionary's* editors many writers of depth and brilliance from the pastoral clinician side of the field.

Among the contributions to *The Dictionary*, it is no surprise that the contribution "Military Service" is a paean to cooperation between the government and religious institutions. Mention is made of "the men (sic) in uniform." The most jingoistic citizen would be comfortable with the contribution. Nowhere in *The Dictionary* is there any mention of dissent from national war policy, of pacifism, or of conscientious objection to military service. And this in a dictionary that includes articles on a very wide range of social issues, from "Teen-age Pregnancy" to "Colostomy."

The Dictionary also seemed to grant a franchise to certain subgroups. For example, partisan Roman Catholics are assigned to write articles on "Priests," "Holy Orders," "Holy Spirit," "Obedience," "Ecclesiology," "Promising," "Self-examination," "Shrines," and "Celibacy." The suggestion that the only Christian priests are

Roman Catholic is an affront to Anglicans, Orthodox, and others. The sanitized explanation of indulgences is an affront to Luther and the Reformation. The article "Promising" suggests that only the sick and immoral abandon vows of marriage or celibacy. This is not to say that each of the Roman Catholic contributors was a religious partisan, but it is to say that too many of them were.

Similarly, fundamentalists from Jerry Falwell's Liberty University were granted the franchise to write uncritically on certain subjects, such as "Moral Majority," and "Christian Therapy Units." The contribution "Parents/Parenthood" expounds on how Christian parents rear their children. One wonders what Jewish or Buddhist parents might do that was different.

The contribution entitled "Cruelty/Sadistic Behavior" mentions only child abuse, and mostly sexual abuse at that. It was the fad of those decades. No reference is made to Adolf Hitler, to the Marquis de Sade, or to Senator Joseph McCarthy. Thus this entry has the effect of fanning the flames of the then current hysteria over the alleged sexual abuse of children, which was the rage in the final two decades of the 20th century. It was an irruption of public hysteria far more damaging than the 17th century Salem witch trials. But it was every bit as fanciful in its creation of "evidence," with stories of children mouthing tales of Satanic possession, claiming to have been forced to drink blood, urine, and to eat feces, and of being forced to sacrifice infants. None of the many accused persons across the country were executed, but a great many suffered interminable prison sentences as well as permanent damage to their reputations and their ability to make a living. No entry in this dictionary is more egregious than this one.

Christian Science was assigned to a Christian Scientist who produced an entirely non-critical piece. Dream Interpretation was given to Jungians as if no one but Jungians had any use for dreams, and by implication disputed the fact that Freud produced the monumental work on dreams, more substantive than Jung's contributions to the subject.

James Fowler was assigned to write on "Faith" and "Faith Development Research" as if no one else had anything to say on the subject or to take exception to Fowler's thesis. The completely uncritical contribution should have been labeled "Fowler on Fowler."

"Sexism" and "Feminist Therapy" make tendentious claims. The reader is informed that male counselors have limited success with women because men are oppressors. It further claims that women are innocent of any reverse sexism, that men invented such a claim, and that women are innocent of any wish to dominate men or discriminate against them. This contribution is a real howler.

Martin Thornton's contribution, "Spiritual Direction" and "Spiritual Director," trivializes pastoral counseling and asserts the superiority of spiritual direction. In this instance, Thornton is somewhat neutralized, blessedly, by Alan Jones' excellent contribution, "Spiritual Direction and Pastoral Care," giving the subject some balance.

On the subject of sexuality there are a number thoughtful and useful contributions. They are balanced though by a number of curiously tendentious articles as well as a number of very strange omissions. For example, the category "Sexual Revolution" does not appear at all. There is a passing aside, however, on "the lie of [sexual] liberation." Blessedly, James Lapsley in "Moral Dilemmas in Pastoral Perspective" refers at least tangentially to open marriage, and J.C. Wynn on "Marriage" refers to "alternate marital styles." The inquiring pastor who stumbles on these brief asides will get no further help in this dictionary on the subject of the Sexual Revolution or its very significant consequences. Needless to add, my own writings on the Sexual Revolution from the 1970s and 80s, which had appeared in some of Robert Rimmer's collections, and in national newspapers, as well as the widely read journal *Christianity and Crisis*, found no mention in *The Dictionary*.

Homosexuals might have wished to have had similar neglect rather than the beating they take in the article "Sexual Variety, Deviance, and Disorder," written by John M. Vayhinger, Ph.D. He contends authoritatively that homosexuality is a matter of personal choice and conditioning—hence, a clear matter of unethical conduct. Vayhinger goes on to argue that the removal of homosexuality from the American Psychiatric Association's list of mental disorders, in 1968, was a mistake effected by the political muscle of gay-rights groups. He then adds that homosexuality is "uniformly condemned" in the Bible, oblivious to counterarguments, such as those of the persuasive John Boswell. The author writes that homosexuality can be cured through repentance and psychotherapy, at least for those homosexuals who "cooperate" with their therapists. Vayhinger writes, "It is only when the individual is convinced that his or her perversion is inborn and refuses to cooperate in counseling or to admit that his or her behavior is immoral or a perversion, that it remains fixed in the personality, just as any other neurotic attitude." Vayhinger is entitled to polemical opinions, but this is a dictionary, and he made it a soapbox. The editor's note pointing out that these opinions are subject to dispute is well advised, but certainly not sufficient enough of a disclaimer.

All in all, *The Dictionary* is a mélange of extraordinary brilliance and the most ignorant unsubstantiated froth. Given the date of its publication, 1990, its double talk was understandable. *The Dictionary* was certainly an accurate reflection of the overheated crosscurrents and contradictions of the clinical pastoral movement in the last quarter of the 20th century. In that regard, it is a very faithful document. *The Dictionary* was revised in 2005, and undoubtedly scrubbed clean of some of its more egregious errors. An interesting project for some graduate theological student would be an investigation of the items that the editors thought needed changing, those they thought not, and what the changes actually were.

In any case the 1990 edition of *The Dictionary* will remain as a permanent monument to the kind of thinking and the values of the wider clinical pastoral movement near the end of the 20th century, with all its brilliance and its many warts, as well.

20.
THE CREATION OF THE COLLEGE OF PASTORAL SUPERVISION AND PSYCHOTHERAPY (CPSP)

After four issues of the *ACPE Underground Report,* and with no substantive response from the ACPE leadership, calls began to be made by various persons for the creation of a new, alternative certifying and accrediting body. No action was taken for two years, until the fall 1989 ACPE Annual Conference in Houston. By then the ACPE UR had an authentic Advisory Panel, chaired by Bill Russell. The Panel met twice during the ACPE meeting, with about thirty persons participating in one meeting or another. A consensus was reached by 13 supervisors supporting a proposal by Bob Pearce that we should create a new organization.[31] The stated motivation of the consensus was the profound malaise commonly shared about the health of both the ACPE and the AAPC. The proposed name of the new body was "The College of Pastoral Counselors and Supervisors," and the date was set for the weekend of March 17, and the place, somewhere on the East Coast. I was authorized to invite interested persons to come together at some agreed-upon location. I asked Perry Miller, a fellow ACPE supervisor, and Robert Claytor, an AAPC pastoral counselor to join me in devising a plan. Thus, on a snowy day in December, the three of us met in Roanoke, Virginia, and issued an invitation to all interested parties to gather at Phoebe Needles Conference Center near Roanoke, Virginia, on the weekend of March 17, 1990, to decide our course of action.

Only about nine persons registered, and we were on the boundary of cancelling. We decided, however, to follow through. As it turned out, 15 persons attended along with the president of ACPE, Julian Byrd, who came to encourage us not to take any formal action.[32] After a long discussion over three days, the 15 decided unanimously to create the College of Pastoral Education and Psychotherapy. (Byrd did not participate in the decision.) We spent Sunday morning brainstorming about what should be contained in a covenant that would bond us. I took notes on the wide range of spontaneous thoughts about what should be contained in a covenant. I went home and put these notes into the form of the Covenant that was approved by the leadership and has remained virtually unchanged since 1990.

But when I got home, I realized that our acronym would be CPEP, much to my horror. When we next reconvened, in July in Little Rock, the members agreed to revise the name to the College of Pastoral Supervision and Psychotherapy, and the more felicitous sounding CPSP. The change was motivated by euphonics, not by any debate over the distinction between supervision and education. At that point in history none of us were in tune with the dialectic of training vs. education that is now so deeply and troublesomely embedded in our history. We committed ourselves to be a volunteer organization and agreed that we would pay salaries only for administrative support performed by non-certified persons. We have continued to adhere to that commitment.

We committed also to a chapter model of organization as opposed to a corporate bureaucracy. We proposed that Chapters be the context for continuing, annual recertification of members. The vision of the Chapter, a small group of not more than a dozen persons, derived from my experience on the ACPE Certification Committee for over a decade. What I came to learn in that experience through meetings held twice a year at the national level and the same number of times at the regional level, was how valuable such an experience was, not so much for the person being examined, but for the committee members themselves. Spending two or more days intensely examining supplicants for certification resulted in the examining committee needing to invest in a great amount of time and energy attempting to decipher what it was that we were seeking in a clinical pastoral supervisor. The work of a serious small group engaged in such intense dialogue was enriching beyond anything that took place at the typical annual gatherings of the community, where registrants engaged either in small talk or listening passively to experts presenting long speeches.

Within six months, CPSP had five Chapters functioning: Chapel Hill convened by Perry Miller; Atlanta by Chappell Wilson; San Antonio by Gene Allen; Washington, D.C., by John Teer; and Lexington by Ben Bogia.

Since organizing in 1990, we have as yet been unable to establish a collegial, face-to-face meeting with the leadership of ACPE. Our existence seems to have represented some continuing narcissistic injury to the ACPE, from which they cannot seem to recover. The AAPC, on the other hand, has been more collegial, especially in recent years, but unfortunately it has been in broad retreat as an organization. State licensure has weakened AAPC and in some states rendered its existence mostly redundant.

At the time of our creation as a credentialing community in 1990, we were only dimly aware of the history of the clinical pastoral training movement. The names of Boisen, Dunbar, Cabot, and other early leaders, carried only vague associations. It is safe to say that we were relatively ignorant of our history. By this time, few of us had paid any attention to Robert Charles Powell, self-appointed historian of the movement, if indeed we had even heard of him. That was to come later. But unbeknownst to us at the time, we were reenacting history. By the seat of our pants we were reasserting the philosophy and values of Anton Boisen and Helen Flanders Dunbar in the face of the more currently powerful philosophy of Richard Cabot.

The original CPSP Covenant from 1990 follows, which has been edited but remains substantially unchanged:

THE COVENANT

CPSP Diplomates see themselves as spiritual pilgrims seeking a truly collegial professional community. Their calling and commitments are therefore first and last theological. Diplomates covenant to address one another and to be addressed by one another in the profound theological sense. They commit to being mutually responsible to one another for their professional work and destiny. Thus they organize themselves in such a way that each participates in a relatively small group call a Chapter, consisting of approximately a dozen persons. Matters that are typically dealt with in other certifying bodies by certification, accreditation, and judiciary commissions will be dealt with in Chapters.

CPSP will certify persons only, not institutions. Therefore, teaching or counseling programs directed by CPSP Diplomates are by definition certified and accredited by CPSP. CPSP Diplomate certification is contingent on satisfactory participation in a CPSP Chapter. Minimal acceptable standards for participation will be decided by the respective Chapters themselves.

Diplomates commit themselves to a galaxy of shared values that are as deeply held as they are difficult to communicate. "Recovery of soul" is perhaps an appropriate metaphor that sums up these shared values. Diplomates place a premium on the significance of relationships among themselves. They value personal authority and creativity. They believe they should "make a space" for one another and stand ready to midwife one another in their respective spiritual journeys. Because they believe that life is best lived "by grace," they believe it essential to guard against becoming invasive, aggressive, or predatory toward each other. They believe that persons are always more important than institutions, and that even the institution of CPSP itself must be carefully monitored lest it take on an idolatrous character.

CPSP intends to travel light, to own no property, to accumulate no wealth, and to create no bureaucracy. Money, property, prestige, and power are viewed as detrimental to the life of our collegial community. Should a paid staff of any kind be employed they should be directly responsible to those they serve.

In recent years, in reaction to the continuing success of CPSP, the ACPE and its subsidiaries circled the wagons to create a block of organizations under their hegemony. They wrote a weak document labeled "The Common Standards" and declared themselves adherents to its principles. One of their principles, for example, is the requirement of a five-year review of competence, which is wholly inadequate. CPSP has an annual review of competence.

"The Common Standards" document is substantively quite thin. CPSP easily qualifies, with much to spare. Nevertheless, CPSP requested to join the Common Standards group since the label "Common Standards" was in use as public relations slogan. CPSP was denied admission to the group led by ACPE. The denial was based on no qualitative assessment, but merely on political grounds. No judgment was made about CPSP standards. Thus the ACPE now informs the public that "CPSP does not subscribe to the Common Standards." What it should properly say to the public is that CPSP was refused admission to the self-designated and self-authorizing Common Standards group led by ACPE in an effort by ACPE to corner the clinical pastoral training market. And further, it should confess that ACPE now uses that refusal of admission to substantiate a libelous claim that CPSP lacks substantive standards. This is a sleazy public relations ploy contrived by a former CEO of the HealthCare Chaplaincy Network and found subsequently to be useful to the ACPE and APC. The Common Standards group has no function other than touting its own legitimacy and denigrating its competition.

The posture of ACPE toward CPSP is reminiscent of the contentious and dismissive posture of the dominant medical profession in relation to osteopathic medicine that emerged late in the 19th century. For most of a century, physicians with M.D. degrees blocked doctors of osteopathic medicine (D.O.s) from practicing their discipline. Osteopathic medicine proposed a slightly different posture in the practice of medicine. At the beginning of the 20th century, only four states allowed osteopathic medical practice. By now the war between M.D.s and D.O.s seems to be mostly over, and M.D.s no longer have a lock on the medical profession from the perspective of civil authorities. M.D.s and D.O.s now treat each other generally with professional respect. The religious leaders of the ACPE are as yet a long way from acknowledging the possibility that anyone outside the reach of their authority could be considered competent in the clinical pastoral field.

21.
THE BATTLE OF BRECKENRIDGE

In November of 1991, the ACPE held its annual meeting in Breckenridge, Colorado. It was an astonishing meeting. The males again took an unfriendly licking, to put it mildly. The speakers seemed all to be women. The previous annual meeting, in Baltimore, led me to be certain that the creation of CPSP was the proper and necessary course of action. If there had been any residual doubt, the annual meeting in Breckenridge would have resoundingly dispelled it.

The usually sensible Rosemary Radford Ruether started off the Breckenridge meeting by pronouncing a negative assessment of the writings of Robert Bly, Sam Kean, and other males for their participation in what was then characterized as "the male movement" and for what she called their hostile stance toward women. As an inveterate heterosexual, I personally had never participated in any of those all-male conferences, where men gathered for drumming and other exercises. I cannot imagine anything more boring than such men-only meetings, and I had no desire to get away from women. I did have the impression that the male movement, so-called, was a response to radical feminism and perhaps was important to some men. Though Reuther is articulate and generally fair enough about the problems women have with men, she seemed quite unaware of problems that men might be having with women. That's perhaps understandable. It is easier to fathom one's own problems than to identify with another's. However, this posture led to quite a one-sided discussion. The women's argument seemed to be that women should gather themselves together to consider gender problems, but that men have no business doing any such thing.

But it was Karen Lebacqz who was the real firebrand of this meeting. Lebacqz was Professor of Ethics at the Pacific School of Religion. Her assigned task was to enlighten members of the meeting about the nature of the soul of clinical pastoral training. She was at some disadvantage from the start, it seems, in that there was no indication that she had ever been involved in clinical pastoral training or any of its organizations. How would she know about the soul of a pastoral clinician?

We should add parenthetically that numerous characterizations were scattered through her speech of clinical pastoral supervision as a Christian undertaking, rooted in the body of Christ. That must have been a real shock to the several Jews and other religious non-Christians present at the meeting, some of whom were full dues-paying and certified members of ACPE. Even her reference to the clinical training community as "God's community on earth" was a characterization to which many clinicians would take exception.

As Lebacqz warmed up to her charge, she proceeded to berate male supervisors for their "notorious reputations" as persons who violate ethical norms of sexuality. She was, of course, correct that the clinical training movement from the beginning was rooted in a countercultural take on sexual values and behavior. The movement, indebted very much to Freud, was tarred with the same brush as was the psychoanalytic movement. But Lebacqz did not appear knowledgeable about that history. She focused entirely on current alleged unethical male misbehavior.

Lebacqz proceeded to trash male clinical pastoral supervisors as if they were a tribe of psychopaths. To make her point, she described a vignette of a male supervisor whom she called typical. In the first supervisory appointment this typical male supervisor requested that the female trainee disclose her sexual history. When she demurred, he went on to disclose his own sexual history in vivid detail, indicating finally that he was at that point experiencing an erection. Now, it is of course possible that this vignette offered by Lebacqz was a factual account of an actual supervisory encounter. However, the notion that such inept, antisocial, and boorish behavior is or ever was typical of supervisory behavior in general was a scurrilous assault on the entire clinical pastoral community. Had such an account been presented to the ACPE—or the CPSP—as an ethics complaint, the supervisor in question would have been severely punished and perhaps relieved of his credentials. Several male supervisors have lost credentials for much less egregious violations. Lebacqz presented what is referred to as the proverbial straw man attack: First you create an extreme fabrication, label it as typical, then attack the object of your scorn until it or the entire community is discredited.

If Lebacqz had wished to present extreme cases of human misbehavior, such as her supervisor calling attention to his own erection, she should have in all fairness also shared an equally unusual vignette of, say, a seductive female trainee exposing herself. An aggressive female trainee can be so irresistibly seductive as to test the resolve of most any male. Such encounters are not typical by any means, but they certainly have been known to occur, people being who they are.

But Lebacqz had a political agenda and was not interested in serious or thoughtful reflection on the problems between men and women. She boldly announced her political remedy: "Certify more women! We don't hear stories of sexual exploitation by women." I am surprised that the walls of the conference room did not scream out in protest at such a construct. And where were the men in that meeting? What were they thinking? They were missing in action.

Lebacqz was of course quite wrong. The principal crime of males at that time was not that they were sexually assaulting female trainees with their erections. In earlier generations there may have been some of that. Their principal crime at the point Lebacqz was speaking was that most of them were immobilized in their pathological passivity, their fear of sexuality, and their fear of women. The voices of men in this Breckenridge dialogue were inaudible. The men were out to lunch. The male supervisors took this beating from Lebacqz lying down. They had nothing to say, vividly demonstrating their impotence even while being accused by Lebacqz of being aggressively priapic.

Lebacqz went further. In cases where women accuse men of sexual abuse, the traditional burdens of proof should be revised, she argued. Women are more likely to be telling the truth in such cases because it is so difficult to bring forward such charges. This was a proposal to reverse commonly accepted and well-tested standards of due process in the favor of women. In fact, what Lebacqz was proposing was to give virtual carte blanche to every shrew and Jezebel in the community. Then they would have the power to destroy any male of their choosing.

To her credit, Lebacqz is not of the pious Phil Turner's abstemious school of sexual ethics where nothing is permissible (himself excluded) except sex within the confines of monogamous matrimony. Lebacqz is a liberal. In cases where the pastor or clinical supervisor is a woman, she takes a very liberal position on sexual behavior. In cases where a woman is pastor and her lover is a male parishioner, her concern is that the male may reassert his accustomed phallic authority. It seems that sexual boundaries are not her concern. It's the phallus. Whoever has the penis is prima facie culpable. Lebacqz authenticated herself as a card-carrying male basher.

Following Lebacqz's speech, a woman conference member stood and asked, in a voice dripping with earnest concern, "How are men going to be healed?"

Then a very refreshing voice of another woman spoke and reminded Lebacqz that the ACPE was not a Christian organization. She followed that by wondering out loud how women could avoid being seen as bitches from hell. As used to be said in my childhood, "Give that lady a box of Mars Bars!" On second thought, give her two.

I, too, have argued for certifying more women supervisors, but not because they are more competent or more virtuous than men. Males and females need each other. I believe the ideal is a 50–50 ratio of men and women in the ranks of clinical supervisors. I concur with Karl Barth's injunction to Christian churches that there should be no single gender groups in a religious community. Male and female need each other. So says Barth.

Immediately following the speech by Lebacqz, the new President of ACPE, Cathy Turner, spoke. She declared that the principal focus of her impending two-year term as president would be the problem of sexual exploitation by supervisors. Read "male supervisors." No one ever heard of a woman being charged with sexual exploitation. Thus it was declared that the ACPE would be shifting to an all-out war against male sexual misbehavior. Not a peep was heard in response from any male present.

An incident of unintended humor followed. As was the custom, outgoing President Julian Byrd presented Anton Boisen's personal cane to incoming President Cathy Turner, a symbol of the handing over of the authority of the office. This was a long-standing tradition, the symbol of the office of president. Never mind that the cane was about all that was left of Boisen in the clinical pastoral movement by this time. His writings were not read in the community. His books were out of print. He was rarely referred to except in a pro forma sense, as a significant early leader of the clinical pastoral movement and an also ran to Richard Cabot, M.D.

Cathy Turner and the radical feminists weren't comfortable with the image of a woman president carrying around such a phallic symbol of the office as a cane. So a phalanx of feminists appeared on stage, unscheduled officially, to present Turner with an additional new symbol of the office of president, a fairy wand. Their hearts were in the right place, but their brains were obviously in neutral.

Symbols are tricky things. Was the fairy wand a little phallus to go with the big phallus, the cane? Or was it a clitoral symbol to pair with the phallic symbol? As the wand was displayed, the presenter made comments about the crystals implanted in the fairy wand to represent the feminine, but that did not ring any bells. It made the wand rather more of a malaprop. If the women had been thinking, instead of reacting, they might have come up with a truly feminine symbol, perhaps a sash as is bestowed on the president of Mexico, for example. Something circular and embracing might have provided some complementarity for the phallic cane of Boisen, thus symbolizing the union of male and female. The Hindu Shiva lingam does just that, placing the rod-like phallic symbol in a cup representing the female pudendum. But in suggesting this, my assumption is that such a union of male and female might be desired, a dubious assumption in the context of the animosity toward heterosexuality current in the ACPE at the time. An inordinate number of these new women leaders were homosexual, and it can be assumed that they had no interest in the union of male and female. Perhaps their unconscious assumption was to place the clitoris in conflict with the phallus, in a David and Goliath fashion, with the hope for a winner and a loser. And of course, the loser would be the big one, the one without the crystals.

The subsequent President of ACPE was an African-American male. The cultural stereotype of African-American male sexuality being what it is, a few psyches must have flinched to see this man peddling a cane *and* a fairy wand. I was not in attendance at his inauguration, or at any subsequent ACPE meeting, but my imagination was active as I wondered what he did with the two symbols of his office. Did he carry them around in one hand, or one in each hand? I am told that both the fairy wand and the cane are still passed on to each incoming ACPE president. And these clinical supervisors are alleged to be minor experts in human psychology. Go figure.

The intense and irrational rage against the male by so many women, often by otherwise quite rational women, is a puzzle. It surpasses even the typical rage of Native Americans and African Americans over the abuse they suffered from European Americans. I speculate that the insensitivity and irrationality of this rage in ACPE stems from unconscious material related in part to the physicality of male and female sexual relations. The sexual act physically replicates in certain ways the harsh domination of social relations. God—or nature—has embedded in male-female sexual congress elements of force and bloodshed, even in the context of love and equity. A soft penis cannot do anything. To complete the act of love requires hardness, from the male, and from the woman—malleability, and bloodshed. Such physical and biological realities and discrepancies must rattle the psyches of women who are hypersensitive about being dominated in a larger sense by males. What other possible explanation could there be for the kind of irrationality and rage exhibited by the ACPE women toward men in Breckenridge?

Karl Barth had argued strongly that men and woman must answer to each other for their existence, and that single genders are a form of religious disobedience. It seems that males in the clinical pastoral movement finally realized this in the latter 20th century, and opened widely the ACPE community to women. In response, the women of ACPE sought not community, but payback.

22.
THE GENIUS OF DONALD CAPPS

Donald Capps was, in the latter part of the 20th century and early 21st century, the preeminent academic authority on pastoral counseling in the country. He succeeded Seward Hiltner, in 1981, as Professor of Pastoral Theology at Princeton Seminary. Capps was also very much in the mold of Hiltner. He was not a practicing clinician professionally, but he became the prime intellectual resource for clinicians in his lifetime. He was an astonishingly prolific writer, and often on the cutting edge.

Donald Capps was also a personal friend of mine. I have many letters from him from the days before cyber space, and some email subsequently when he belatedly got into cyber communication. Capps was a self-declared sociophobe. He was averse to social gatherings and to small talk especially. Inviting him to dinner or to a party was a waste of time. He could typically be spotted in some fast food joint like Dunkin' Donuts writing as he drank his coffee. That way he could be in the company of people but not have to relate to them socially. Capps was also a poet and especially enjoyed writing doggerel or limerick poems with an iconoclastic orientation. He also had a commitment to justice. When Don Browning scurrilously trashed my book, *The Poisoning of Eros,* with an ad hominem suggesting that I was immoral, Capps wrote me saying that I ought to file an ethics complaint against him.

Most importantly, Capps squared the circle for followers of Boisen. He linked the healing work of Jesus with that of Freud in a monumental monograph published in 2008. Capps persuasively argued that some, and likely all, of Jesus' cures were of the same order as Freud's. No magic. No deus ex machina. He argued that Jesus worked entirely as a human being among other human beings. The monograph is entitled *Jesus the Village Psychiatrist*.

Capps supports his thesis with a review of Jesus' healing methodology and a detailed examination of a particular case of Freud's, that of Elizabeth von R. Elizabeth's was a case of what is now popularly referred to as psychosomatic paralysis, more professionally known as conversion or somatoform disorder. And Freud was able to cure her, or should we say more modestly that after consultations with Freud her paralysis disappeared. As was Freud's approach, he listened and eventually made some associations or connections, and the patient who could not walk was then able to walk, and even dance. Echoes of Jesus.

Elizabeth's story was that her beloved sister had been bedridden, dying of cancer, and Elizabeth cared for her during her last days, assisted by her sister's husband, her brother-in-law. In the course of the care, Elizabeth would often join her brother-in-law for an afternoon walk in the park in order to take a break from the sickroom. Elizabeth began to fantasize what she would do when her sister was gone, and also what her brother-in-law would do without a wife. Naturally she fantasized that she might marry him herself. This thought, appealing on the face of it, created feelings of guilt that she would benefit from her sister's demise. Her feelings of guilt were apparently intense and seemingly were buried by her in the recesses of her psyche.

Freud's interpretation was that Elizabeth unconsciously developed her paralysis in order to put an end to her afternoon walks with her brother-in-law, walks that stirred her fantasies of marrying him, and consequently her guilt. Her paralysis would thus distract her from her fantasies about her brother-in-law and thus diminish her feelings of guilt over the potential for benefiting from her sister's death.

After Freud discharged Elizabeth he wondered how she might be doing. (One of the disadvantages of being a physician therapist, unlike a pastoral therapist, is the lack of a warrant to pursue patients, to discover their progress or lack thereof.) Freud thus arranged surreptitiously to attend a social event in Vienna where he had reason to believe Elizabeth would also be in attendance. He encountered her there as he expected. She swept past him, vigorously dancing a waltz. She eventually married, but she did not marry her sister's widower. The woman who was unable to walk was now able to dance, thanks to Freud.

Capps' argument is that this was precisely the kind of healing that Jesus was engaged in, curing what is popularly known as psychosomatic illness. And the ancient texts are fully congruent with this argument. Virtually all of the healing narratives, with the exception of the severing and restoration of Peter's ear, are theoretically within the bounds of psychosomatic cures. Certainly there are no reported cures that are unambiguously magical or outside the bounds of the psychosomatic. No one, for example, was restored to life who was clearly decapitated. There is not much a psychotherapist can do with someone whose head has been severed from the body.

Furthermore, according to the texts, Jesus was teaching his disciples to work with disturbed and troubled people in the same manner in which he was working. As we know from history, it didn't take long for Christians to forget all this and to resort to magical thinking and hocus-pocus as a replacement for pastoral psychotherapy. Thus in time it came to be believed that Jesus could do magical cures simply because he was a god in mufti.

When Capps published his monograph, Boisen had of course been dead for almost half a century. But certainly he would have rejoiced to know of Capps' thesis if he could have lived that long. Perhaps Capps' preeminence in the field of pastoral care and counseling will in time come to inspire a resurrection of the Boisen vision.

So far, Capps' thesis does not seem to have found much traction in the current discourse. The picture of Jesus in this generation is either Christendom's typical one, of a god in mufti parading around Palestine pretending to be a human being, or a typically agnostic one, of a person who may have lived in history but whose deeds were exaggerated and who no longer has any relevance to the real world. Unfortunately neither Jesus nor Freud nor Boisen have much currency in modern times. But the arc of history sometimes has a way of bending back to matters of import and of substance.

Unfortunately for us all, Capps died suddenly in 2015, at the age of 75, from injuries sustained in an automobile accident. His death was a great loss to the human community, and to me personally.

23.
MYRON C. MADDEN

No recollection of the history of clinical pastoral training could be complete without the recollection of Myron Madden. Myron was the "younger brother" to Wayne Oates, in a manner of speaking. Oates was to Madden what Madden was to me, an elder brother from whom the younger received extraordinary wisdom and mentoring. Oates, like Madden, was not much venerated in the Southern Baptist Church to which he belonged. It was reported to me that no one from Southern Baptist Theological Seminary attended Oates' burial service. And when Myron gave the eulogy at Oates' funeral in 1999, his closing words about Oates were, "He came unto his own and his own received him not." The same of course could have been said of Myron as well. The two of them were essentially giant outliers among the Southern Baptists.

I first encountered Myron when I was appointed to work on an ACPE Southwest Regional Certification Committee in the early 1970s. What I discovered was that some members of the region in that era fought to be appointed as members of Myron's subcommittees. Not that they were necessarily interested in the certification process itself, but that the dialogue that ensued with Myron present was better than a graduate seminar. Myron was always ready with a pertinent quote from Shakespeare, Freud, Kierkegaard, or the Bible that was relevant to the issue at hand. Sitting in a committee with Myron was better than a small seminar with Harold Bloom, which I also enjoyed once at Yale, and who so much reminded me of Myron, not least for their mutual love of Shakespeare. Though Myron was, of course, embedded in the pastoral tradition, and Bloom was not, there was extraordinary congruence between the two.

Myron's first wife died in 1981, 33 years before Myron himself died. I did not know her. But I came to know his second wife, Ann. She had been a Baptist missionary in Hong Kong and had returned after long service. She joined Myron's clinical pastoral training program at Baptist Hospital in New Orleans. Myron supervised her. They fell in love and married. I cannot imagine anyone more suited to accompany Myron in his final decades. She was an incomparable blessing to him. Myron liked to say that Ann was his Abishag, the young woman who was sent to enliven King David in his declining years. She certainly did that.

In the early years of CPSP, beginning in 1996, Myron agreed to serve as the Plenary chaplain. In the 1997 Plenary, in Virginia Beach, I was in Myron's small group, whether by chance or design, I no longer recall. A lovely young Methodist woman pastor and pastoral clinician presented her case, as was the regimen for the small groups. What she presented was a puzzling dream that she had. The dream was of her encountering at her front door an aggressive snake that threatened to intrude, frightening her. At the critical moment of the intruder's aggression, her cat attacked the snake and drove it off. After some desultory discussion in the group, which seemed to go nowhere, I suggested that the presenting woman was saved by her pussy. Subsequently, the group discussion went into high gear. I no longer recall the dialogue, but I remember the energy and excitement that ensued, especially from Myron. Freudian that he was, Myron loved working with dreams. After the meeting he wrote me. "The best story of the Plenary was the one of the dream of the attack cat." I thought so too.

I was with Myron on what may have been his last fishing trip in the Gulf off the Louisiana Bayous, a pastime he dearly loved. Chappell Wilson had organized the excursion and was along as well. I brought up the subject of clinical supervisors marrying their trainees, and how in the new morality of the ACPE, that was a severely punishable offense. Myron responded, "They're damned fools." The truth is that Myron himself was not at any risk personally. He was Teflon. No one would have touched him. The moral arbiters of the ACPE only went after the little fish that could not defend themselves. And Myron was no little fish. Of course, the fact of a clinical supervisor marrying a trainee was not actually a moral issue at all. It was declared a moral issue only if the relationship turned sour. A soured heterosexual relationship was typically assessed as consisting of a woman abused by a predatory male. Then it became an instrument for beating up on the heterosexual male.

Myron served CPSP as the regular Plenary Chaplain for about a decade. But in 2006 his hearing deficit became so serious that he could not function conversationally. He sent the following message to the 2006 meeting in Little Rock:

> This is a word to my beloved sisters and brothers in CPSP. That word is to express my regrets of having to miss the annual meeting of CPSP. A couple of weeks ago I crossed the double 8 marker. Age has done what age does to people of my years; it has left me feeble of life and limb. Fortunately its work has been wrought upon the physical and not so much the mental. As a result I am left longing to be at the meeting with you without the ability to circulate among you as in times past.
> I have to accept what has been given, or rather what has been taken away.
> I have struggled to make my ministry one of bringing blessings into the lives of others. But you can never be sure if you have succeeded unless it comes back in the form of some real human affirmation from others. You as a group in CPSP have so affirmed me that I can go in the strength of that gift even as the body stretches toward sundown. Have a great meeting, and I will celebrate down here in the ravages left by Katrina.

Myron lived another seven years. He died on June 4, 2013. He had kept in contact with me by mail. He strongly affirmed life even as little by little it was being taken away. His last letter to me was dated April 29, five weeks before he died. It is hand written and legible, but barely. His wit survived. He reported that he could do almost nothing for himself, and was not even able to dial 911. If he could not laugh at his many slips, he reported, life would be dull indeed. "So many things are laughable," he wrote, "and of course many are not." He reported that Ann, fortunately, has a great sense of humor. Even to the end of his life Myron was still bestowing his blessings.

Myron's funeral was a modest affair. Like Wayne Oates' before him, it did not represent the fullness of Myron's life. The president of CPSP, Brian Childs, attended with me and a handful of other CPSP and several ACPE colleagues.

In my view Myron Madden was spiritual heir to the Wayne Oates tradition. He was also the incommensurable patriarch of CPSP. As Ben Johnson said of Shakespeare when he was gone, "He was not for an age, but for all time."

24.
WAYNE OATES

The position of Wayne Oates in the history of the clinical pastoral training movement is a conundrum. In so many ways he was the most Boisenian of all of the early leaders. He personally trained with Boisen at Elgin State Hospital, in Chicago, in 1944. He wrote his Ph.D. thesis on Freud. In the merger of the four disparate groups in 1967, he brought the largest contingent in under his banner, the Southern Baptist Association for Clinical Pastoral Education. The name of the new organization, ACPE, was the name of his organization with "Southern Baptist" deleted. Arguably it should have been deleted earlier, since a quarter of its certified members were of a religion other than Southern Baptist.

Between 1970 and 1990 I was very active in the ACPE regionally and nationally, and I did not meet Oates at any meeting. Nor do I even remember hearing Oates' name mentioned, except on occasion by Myron Madden, who was a protégé and long-time friend of Oates. I did hear Oates give a lecture once, in the 1970s, at Louisville Baptist Seminary where he was teaching. I recall that he made a comment about the Sexual Revolution, to the effect that Christian pastors would need to make some changes in their customary sexual attitudes if they were going to be effective with people in the new generation. Regrettably, I neglected to approach him personally on the subject, a subject that was very much on my own mind.

At the merger in 1967, the creation of the ACPE, Oates was essentially the kingmaker. And yet there is no evidence that he exercised much authority in that federating process. And he remained for the rest of his life on the fringe of the ACPE. This is something of a puzzle. Yet Oates' story replicates in a sense the life story of Boisen himself, who inaugurated the Council only to abandon it to others two years after its incorporation in 1930 as the Council (literally, CCTTS). And of course, as usually occurs in history, his latter successors eventually, after a decade or so, ran it into the ground, even during Boisen's lifetime. The refusal of the Council to certify Oates in the late 1940s is something that would have dismayed Boisen himself if he knew of it. Does this suggest a peculiar posture toward authority and leadership on the part of Oates? Or was he purposely and quietly silenced in the relatively small community of several hundred clinical supervisors?

Though Oates had the largest contingent of troops at that organizing meeting, Chuck Hall dominated the gathering as chief executive of the Council and was made executive director of the new entity. Arguably Oates should have had the role assigned to Hall. He singlehandedly, it seems, created a large, ecumenical group of psychoanalytically oriented supervisors, mostly in the South. It included the likes of Myron Madden, Don Cabaniss, Richard Young, O. Chappell Wilson, and many other highly creative clinical supervisors. Why Oates moved to the fringe after 1967, or whether he chose isolation, is a puzzle. It is noteworthy that Oates is the only early leader of the movement who now has an eponymous institute in his memory. Perhaps the researchers of that Oates Institute can solve this riddle of Oates' life.

There are several possibilities that would have led to Oates' isolation in the newly forming ACPE community. Oates troops were mostly southerners, three-quarters of them were Baptists, but perhaps most damaging was that they were quite psychoanalytically oriented and unashamedly so. I speculate that the latter was their fatal flaw in the view of the wider group. Oates was out of step with the post-1967 trend in the ACPE. Oates' Ph.D. thesis on Freud was never published. It was written at a time when the psychoanalytic tradition was gradually being expunged from the clinical training movement. From the beginning of the ACPE, the leadership was deconstructing the Boisen vision and its psychoanalytic foundations.

Another possibility—or contributing factor, perhaps—is that Oates envisioned an open community that did not exclude petitioners. Like Boisen, he had a distaste for rejecting or excluding any person who aspired to be supervisor. This was likely due in part to Oates' own rejection at the hands of the Council in the late 1940s. Oates envisioned an organization of pastoral clinicians as an open fellowship, not a bureaucracy focused on prestige, power, money, and property.

And then there is the class factor. Oates was born into dire poverty in the mill town of Greenville, South Carolina. He had the aura of a rough-hewn man, and he never shed that inherited aura in spite of his intellectual prowess and academic success.

In 1993, I began a correspondence with Oates. As I recall, I had written him thanking him for his book, *The Struggle To Be Free*. And I sent him, unsolicited, a copy of my *Poisoning of Eros*. On January 9, 1994, he wrote me the first of five letters I have from him, which I have preserved, all hand-written. He was effusive in his praise of my book. We exchanged a few more letters. The last letter I have from him is dated June 13, 1999. He was then grieving the death of his son, a Vietnam War veteran who suffered terribly from post-traumatic stress. Oates himself died four months later, on October 21.

In his letters Oates was affirming of the creation of CPSP and its stated values. He especially lauded the CPSP Covenant, which seemed to him to call for a fellowship rather than a bureaucracy of money, power, property, and prestige. Oates was one of the most sophisticated thinkers in the history of the clinical pastoral movement. He was more widely read and culturally informed than most of the clinical supervisors I have known. And he was one of the most unrecognized and underappreciated leaders in the clinical pastoral training movement of his generation. I regret that for whatever cause I had so little interface with him while he lived.

25.
ATTACKING THE SEXUAL COUNTERREVOLUTION

In the 1990s the sexual counterrevolution was in full bloom. An hysterical virus was infecting childcare centers throughout the country and a few places abroad. This plague was poisoning relationships between religious leaders and their flocks, particularly women and children. It was a dangerous time to be a heterosexual male, and especially dangerous for a male pastor to be alone with a woman or a child. Nor were women entirely immune to such charges. The hysteria ultimately ruined many women as well as men. False accusations of sexual misbehavior were legion, and there was no easy defense against them. The presumptive predator was always a presumptive liar. This issue was a powerful subtext throughout the clinical pastoral movement as well and was especially motivating in the formation of the CPSP in 1990.

I personally attacked in my newsletter, now renamed *Contra Mundum*, the integrity of the associate dean at Yale Divinity School, Phil Turner, for his duplicity on sexual ethics. He posed as the Episcopal Church's senior authority on sexual ethics. He was an inflexible hard-liner on behalf of traditional sexual rules. And yet, at the same time he pulled off a quickie divorce from his wife of long-standing so that he could marry one of his seminary students, all this within the space of one year. Turner was a genius at having it both ways.

I also inveighed against the bitter negativity of Marie Fortune, whose vendetta against male sexuality poisoned a wide swath of the American religious community in the late 20th century, a poisoning from which we have as yet to recover. But it must be said in all honesty that the churches generally egged on Marie Fortune and paid her good money for spreading this hysteria. She saw a good way to make money and took advantage of it. And the churches and their judicatories, guided by an inexplicable motivation, were willing to cough up large sums of money to hear that the male of the species is an inveterate sexual predator, and beyond that to hear that sexual predators of both genders were lurking behind every tree.

In an effort to counter Marie Fortune and her kind, I proposed 10 axioms or talking points for guidance in assessing and adjudicating alleged sexual violations by clergy. Below is the abbreviated version of my 10 points from "The Current Frenzy Over Sex Abuse by Clergy," *Underground Report,* issue 37, November 1, 1992:

> 1. Actual sexual abuse is difficult to assess. The basic determinative question posed by Marie Fortune, "Did the penis enter the vagina?" will not do.

> 2. The wish to purge the pastoral role of sexuality altogether threatens to destroy pastoral ministry itself. Ministry is actually a form of sex education, in the broadest sense. African-American pastors understand this. In the early Christian church the mouth-to-mouth kiss of peace was sacramental, and undoubtedly sexually charged.

> 3. A sexual relationship between a minister and a parishioner is the rule rather than the exception. Male ministers seeking a spouse will look first in their own congregations, and when they marry, their wives will be members of the congregation. This is universal practice from time immemorial.

> 4. The truest benchmark for a sexual relationship that is not exploitative is peership. Adult-child sex is the extreme in lack of peership.

> 5. The covert assumption in much discussion of sexual behavior is that sex is a dirty business, and that abstinence is somehow a special virtue. The biblical tradition blessedly counters this covert malign assumption.

> 6. Recent literature makes no distinction between taboo and ethics. The length of women's dresses, for example, is a changing cultural

taboo, as are many other modes of behavior. It has no relation to ethics.

7. The presumption of sexual purity is not a helpful marker for competent leadership. Many of our most effective political and religious leaders have been those most willing to flout middle-class sexual mores.

8. Much of what passes for indignation against sex abuse by clergy is simply covert and unconscious rage against the phallus. Who has ever heard of sex abuse charges brought against a homosexual woman?

9. Any discussion of sexual ethics devoid of humor ought to be avoided. It was God, after all, who invented sex, and not only for the purpose of procreation. Sex was invented for our pleasure, and also to make us look absurd. Accepting the absurdity of sex is a requirement for mental health.

10. Liberation in all its forms should be promoted, and that includes sexual liberation. But liberation is not license to abuse others. It is freedom from taboo and meaningless social rules. True liberation is not only for the self, but for self and others as well.

26.
ANONYMOUS

The following letter to the editor of the *Underground Report* was published in issue 39, February 1993. It was one of the most poignant and insightfully confessional descriptions of the problem of sexual boundaries that I have ever read. The writer, a woman, captured in words the spirit of the clinical training movement as few persons of either gender have. She described so well both the chaos and creativity of clinical pastoral training itself. The writer's humane posture toward boundary crossings is instructive to anyone with a soul. She describes her own boundary crossings with sensitivity and humanity, while remaining aware of the potential problems that may follow, and faithfully attending to them. The author's name was withheld by request:

> ... For me that summer of Clinical Pastoral Education was a watershed event in my life. I was one of only four women, sexually repressed as only a "good girl" from the fifties could be, charged by feminism and its promise with some autonomy, overwhelmed by my assignment to the hospital burn unit, vaguely discontent with my gay husband's emotional distance, and surrounded by a score of sensitive, spiritually aware (or so I thought), straight men. Then you add all those existential sessions where we were poked and prodded by supervisors and forced to look into nooks and crannies previously untouched, it is no wonder that sexual energy bounced off the walls. Eventually (after the training course) both the women in my group landed in bed with our supervisor. Of the four of us three ended our marriages within a year.
>
> I do not mean to make my supervisor appear professionally suspect. He did act appropriately. He and the other woman fell in love and went through several painful years dealing with that. Her marriage, like mine, was ninety percent over before she ever entered CPE. As

to my having sex with him over a year later, the poor guy didn't stand a chance. If we're talking about balances of power, a 38-year-old woman who has unleashed the shackles of sexual repression could probably provide enough energy to heat the entire east coast. I spent a year investigating every possibility available to me short of children, dead bodies, and animals. I was admittedly crazy as a loon, but it was fun in a Twilight Zone way.

I just don't want you to think there was a CPE supervisor out there 'taking advantage' of innocent women. It may not have been the smartest thing either of us did, but I certainly was no victim.

In my experience CPE is not destructive to marriages, nor is it destructive to women, though I would say that I found it not as sensitive to female thought or morality as it could have been. Too much Kohlberg and not enough Gilligan to be simplistic, or maybe more Paul of Tarsus than Mary Magdalene. The point, though, is that CPE was designed to open us up, challenge our beliefs, and jolt us substantially. It certainly sent me into eight years of therapy which might be the healthy and constructive way to handle the confusion and doubt and anxiety it can induce.

As this sexual abuse/victim ridiculousness escalates, I would think that CPE programs are extraordinarily vulnerable. I have always believed that religiosity and repressed sexuality are Siamese Twins, and when supervisors feed the sexual sibling, the churchy one attacks to save itself. Now we have a nation egging on the sick half and encouraging folks to substitute blame for self-discovery.

Many women who are church professionals are politically correct feminists of the 'Take Back the Night' variety, and while I too am a feminist, and don't ever want men to feel that "boys will be boys" defends their insensitive behavior towards us (i.e. the Tail Hook Scandal), I do believe that repressing sexual energy is both impossible and, more importantly, boring. We've got to learn as we struggle for some genuine power in a world which gives us little, how to do it on our own terms with our own values, but with some understanding and tolerance for the ways of men. Backing men into corners and screaming "rape/abuse" is not a great way to negotiate. Maybe all of this is a sick and horribly misguided attempt by the powerless to feel more in control. The tragedy is that so many good and innocent people are being destroyed in the process.

As I reread this letter again, a quarter century later, it touched me deeply. I was brought up short as memories flooded me of the yeasty spirit of clinical pastoral training that I had entered in the 1960s, and how far the clinical pastoral community has drifted since that time. Perhaps it is not too hyperbolic to say that clinical pastoral training has for the most part morphed through my lifetime from a yeasty, redemptive, radical, and life-changing experience (as the letter writer above describes) into a lifeless paint-by-numbers project. And the cause of this regressive transformation has largely been the rage of women allied with male cowardice. Thus instead of living into our newly discovered selves, including our sexual selves—as the letter writer has—women have turned their anger on men and successfully disempowered both themselves and men in general. And it cannot be forgotten that this feminist rage has been aided and abetted by gross fear, cowardice, and panic on the part of men generally.

A cursory review of the files does not reveal the original of this letter. Perhaps a more thorough search will uncover it. Or perhaps in my effort to protect her anonymity I destroyed the original. The author must be about 60 years old by now. I would love for this wise and articulate woman to contact me again and share with me her journey, now a generation later. I hope she still lives and prospers.

27.
AND FROM THE DISTAFF SIDE

In the same month, the *Underground Report* received a different kind of letter, also articulate and far more representative of the mood of the times, from a prominent officer at the Commission for Women, Evangelical Lutheran Church in America. Though she identified herself publicly in the original letter, written on Lutheran Church stationery, and did not request anonymity, I will assume her views may have evolved enough that she would now not want to be personally linked to the following tirade she wrote in 1993. So I will withhold her name in what I consider an act of kindness. Some of the references in the letter below relate to the full article in the *Underground Report,* issue 37.

Dear Mr. Blessedly Erect Phallus,

Such a pleasure to read your farce, "The Current Frenzy Over Sex Abuse by Clergy." Whoever said that pastoral counselors have no sense of humor have obviously never seen the *Underground Report.* At first I thought this was a serious essay...but by paragraph 6, I got the picture at last. (Oh, the relishing of that lacerated hymen---you cad, you.) By paragraph 8, I was rolling in the aisles. ("Sexual liaisons...never become a problem until the participants decide they are a problem" or in the next paragraph, Potiphar's Wife. And then, further on down the page, the daring takeoff on the 1940s Roman Catholic seminary training picture of the "young Roman Catholic woman who has boasted gleefully of seducing a young priest" - amazing.) And then of course, the "ten Axioms," including the astonishingly cute line put into Marie Fortune's mouth ("Did the penis enter the vagina?") or the fascinating notion that "anyone who knows what sexual abuse looks like...ought to be considered suspect." Or, "a violation is seen to occur only when a sexual liaison turns sour -

the whole world knows this." (Mild little chuckles.) Or again, "any single minister searching for a spouse will rightly look first in the congregation for a candidate." Boffo! Belly laughs! Or again, "written accounts of daily life at Auschwitz contain more humor that all the writings of Fortune and Rutter." What can I say? I haven't laughed like this since I used to read MAD Magazine as a teen, or Paul Krassner (Surely you know the classic scene on Air Force One after the Kennedy assassination, the flavor is the same.) or Lenny Bruce back in the Good Old Days before those "long lines of indicted males" facing committees...This is the humor Norman Mailer might have written if he'd had a sense of humor.

Or maybe even Karl Barth: the theological acumen was breathtaking! What flair, what pizzazz! Hard to separate, sometimes from the dizzying craftsmanship of the comic mind, but that's part of its beauty. What can I say? Except to applaud and commend such foundationally rich and suggestive distinctions as those between "taboo and ethics" (including "to break a taboo can be an act of liberation" but I especially LOVED the notion that "it is almost impossible to separate taboo and ethics.")...with ground-breaking historical generalizations (esp. in point 10, such as "even the limitation of sexual relationship to the marital state is not consistently demanded by much of religious tradition.")...the exegetical daring of "One of the few things the Bible seems consistent about is that a sexual relationship needs no justification, but need only be free of specific prohibitions."

But I won't go on retailing its delights. Instead I want you to know I'm circulating it to all my friends because I'm sure they'll get the same jollies I did. What better way to conclude than by echoing your final glorious sentences, slaying the typical activities of the foolhardy as the proving ground of the courageous. Bingo! Do write, at length, the humorous sexual ethics (with more of those Biblical and historical-theological bases) that will set us all straight. We NEED your work.

An Outrageously Amused Grim Warrior Against Sex Abuse

This very inventive correspondent presents an authentic characterization of the spirit of the times.

28.
A REVELATORY TALE

One of the former executive directors of one of the principal national certifying bodies in the clinical pastoral movement retired from his office, and in retirement undertook part-time clinical pastoral training work on a contract basis. In the course of a freelance training unit he became sexually involved with a trainee, a young married woman. In short order this relationship became troublesome, as anyone could have predicted. Clinical supervision and sexual play are not simultaneously compatible under most, if not all, circumstances. The supervisor quickly came to his senses and sought mediation, forgiveness, and reconciliation. He candidly acknowledged that he had transgressed an important boundary on several counts. In this remarkable act of repentance, with the help of an outside pastoral consultant, he and his wife, along with his trainee and her husband, met together and processed this grievous violation. Astonishingly, all three aggrieved parties eventually accepted his appeal for forgiveness, and the matter was eventually closed, seemingly with no lasting injury to anyone involved. In a rational, caring community, why shouldn't we expect this kind of forgiveness and reconciliation? The amazing aspect of the process was that it could happen at all in the context of a community conflicted over sexuality in general and inflamed by a sexual counterrevolution fueled by rage against males. We speculate that this reconciliation stemmed at least in part from the presumed victim couple being Jewish. Of all the religious traditions in the world, Judaism is the least hysterical and the least neurotic about sexual boundary problems.

Shortly thereafter the supervisor in question moved with his family to another state a great distance away and offered his home to a pair of women who were colleagues in the clinical pastoral community. The pair had just moved to town, having taken new jobs, and were seeking temporary living quarters. They leased the home of the repentant supervisor temporarily, complete with furnishings. In due course the two women penetrated the man's computer and discovered the data of the sexual liaison and its subsequent reconciliation process. Enraged at the behavior of the supervisor, and enraged that he had escaped serious punishment, they themselves filed a third-party ethics complaint against him. The certifying organization processed the complaint, found the supervisor guilty, and removed his credentials for life.

From any reasonable perspective regarding due process, the two women had no standing to file an ethics complaint. They were in no way aggrieved parties, except within the boundaries of their own neuroses. Furthermore, they were arguably guilty of theft. The only rational perspective as to why they took such invasive third-party action is that they harbored resentment that a heterosexual male might find forgiveness and reconciliation after a sexual boundary violation in relation to a woman trainee. This story captures the essence of the sexual cold war taking place between the genders in certain parts of the clinical pastoral community. It reveals the intractable animosities concisely and poignantly. This episode epitomizes the troubled relationship between men and women in the wider clinical pastoral community. The rage among certain women against any male, and their obvious need to punish has poisoned the entire community in this generation.

In the first year of the clinical training movement, which was inaugurated in the summer of 1925, Anton Boisen made a sexually intimate approach toward Helen Flanders Dunbar, his trainee. Boisen reported that she was responsive, but precisely what that meant specifically was not disclosed. However, the irony here is that a principal leader of the clinical pastoral movement was professionally destroyed three-quarters of a century later for the same actions that Boisen himself took earlier.

Wherever persons are in relationship there will always be grievances and boundary violations. In a responsible community, grievances are typically examined and redressed appropriately, and reconciliation sought. This is what much of the clinical pastoral community seems unable to accomplish in the present time, particularly in a case of a heterosexual male crossing a forbidden sexual boundary in relation to a woman.

The punitive action against this notable leader of the clinical pastoral movement, the fruit of female rage and male impotence, epitomizes the moral bankruptcy of the movement after almost a century of history. It takes a twisted soul to seek punishment for two persons who have crossed boundaries seeking love, but who have repented of their violation and been forgiven.

The truth is that the entire clinical pastoral community should have rejoiced that this supervisor and his wife, along with the trainee and her husband, could reach a point of forgiveness and reconciliation without the need to humiliate or degrade anyone for what was a very human act. Crimes of love should be the most forgivable of crimes. Dante knew that. He put the adulterous lovers, Paolo and Francesca, in the first ring of hell, nearest to the exit. That's where crimes of love belong. The perpetrators of crimes of hate, such as those executed by the two female accusers and the compliant clinical pastoral organization, belong much deeper in the reaches of hell. That is where Dante surely would place them.

29.
NOW AT THIS JUNCTURE

Institutional chaplaincy is currently a clinical wasteland. The numbers of hospital chaplains have greatly multiplied many times over since the beginning of the clinical pastoral movement in 1925. However the quality of the work is at best uneven and in general very weak.

A major contributing factor in this deterioration in quality and competency has been the radical shift in the underlying philosophy of chaplaincy. In 1999, the ACPE and the APC decided it was time to erase "pastoral" from its lexicon and replace it with "spiritual." In their campaign to accomplish this, they petitioned the Joint Commission[1] requesting that it delete "pastoral care and counseling" from its directory of auxiliary hospital services and replace the category with "spiritual care." Figuring that all these pastoral authorities in the ACPE and the APC knew what they were doing, the Joint Commission complied. Many, if not most of the hospitals in the country followed suit and renamed their chaplains departments. Interestingly, one of the leaders in this initiative was Joan Hemenway, who at that time was director of pastoral care at the Bridgeport, Connecticut, hospital. Her own hospital board refused to go along with her recommendation to change the name of her department. "Too California," the hospital board countered. One could say that that was a slur against California.

If the pastoral clinicians in 1999 had read any substantive theology, they might not have gone so easily astray. The preeminent theologian of the 20th century, Paul Tillich, had explicitly warned against relying on the category "spirituality" in modern discourse, saying that it was a confusing word, having drifted too far from the meaning it carried in ancient history. But no one was reading Tillich anymore. The seminaries had erased him from their courses, another victory of the radical feminists. Everyone knew by that time that Tillich had been an incorrigibly bad boy sexually. Thus, under feminist pressure, an entire generation of seminarians was steered away from reading both Tillich and Karl Barth, another sexual non-conformist, because of their failures to abide by middle-class sexual standards.

Pastoral care and pastoral counseling carried with them a body of literature, Seward Hiltner being arguably the leading theoretician of pastoral work in the mid-20th century. Spiritual care had no significant literature and still has none, simply because the category has yet to be defined. The result is that spiritual is defined by any speaker according to the speaker's own desires and predilections, a perfect definition of babble, and a platform for raw narcissism.

The most effective antidote to spiritual is clinical. Deriving from the Greek word *klini,* meaning "bed," clinical refers to the body in bed as the focal point of attention. Those who elect to attend to the spiritual do not focus on the body in bed, but on some vaporous something out there, up there.

The APC, currently the largest such certifying body in the country, has the honesty to refrain from identifying itself as a clinically oriented organization or from offering "clinical certification." It merely claims to offer "professional certification." The APC chaplains may be professionals, but they do not have a tradition of functioning as clinicians. More often than otherwise, these chaplains are professional prayer warriors. Generally they function like broad-spectrum evangelists, regardless of their specific religious tradition. Their main objective is to engage in religious conversation with patients. Typically that means enticing patients to pray or to listen to prayers on their behalf. That kind of work doesn't take much training, and certainly not much clinical acumen. It requires the skills of a Fuller Brush salesman.

Demonstrable proof of this evangelistic campaign to promote prayer can be seen in a recently published and highly touted book, *Spiritual Care in Practice: Case Studies in Healthcare Chaplaincy,* edited by George Fitchett & Steve Nolan.[2] This publication purports to display exemplary chaplaincy work. The book consists of nine cases portraying nine chaplains working with their patients. The cases for the most part present embarrassingly poor examples of pastoral work. Most of the chaplains in the collection, some of whom, astonishingly, were said to be engaged in supervising chaplaincy trainees, displayed their own work and exposed themselves as clinically uninformed. Several of them were out and out prayer warriors. That is to say, if they could not get a prayer in during their visit, they felt they had neglected the patient. This book could be called the definitive proof of the current widespread incompetence in institutional chaplaincy as a whole. One must conclude from the evidence in the book that chaplaincy currently is a profession based on fanciful and imaginative activity, unrelated to actual suffering, and bereft of any demonstrable positive results. This kind of chaplaincy will not stand the test of time. It is doomed to oblivion. Though Fitchett and Nolan came out of the theological arena, most of the marquee experts on chaplaincy in recent years have a non-theological background. This is a most peculiar phenomenon. What it represents is something of a mystery. It is as if suddenly most of the principal experts on disease, health, and medical treatment were architects or financial managers. For non-medical people to have a keen interest in medicine and in health is commendable, but it would pass as strange for physicians to be trumped by non-medical laypersons. Yet such is now the case for chaplains. Most of the alleged experts in the field of chaplaincy, and pastoral care and counseling, are untrained clinically.

One of the tactics that these emerging religious experts untrained in pastoral care and counseling resort to now is to change the language. They avoid discussing religion, theology, chaplaincy, pastoral care and counseling, and have adopted the new lingo of spirituality. In the realm of spirituality there are no experts because no one quite knows what is meant by spirituality. Harold Koenig is perhaps the biggest name currently among the nontheologians who have become in the popular mind expert in the work of religious professionals. He is a psychiatrist promoting the oblong blur of spirituality. He somehow presumes that the very mention of spirituality forces persons to their knees in reverence to something, but who knows what. Koenig tells how he encountered a woman with spinal stenosis in irreversible decline who confided her troubles to him, adding that she believed that "no one gets well unless they pray," and she has certainly been praying. But she is not getting well. In fact, she is not going to get well. Rather than entering into the woman's tragically self-condemning dilemma—namely, that she is praying but not getting better—Koenig blows her off on parting, telling her simply to "keep on praying." He must have been in a hurry. A psychiatrist promoting such banality, and who is so unable to listen and to hear what a patient is saying, should lose his license to practice. Obviously, Koenig never studied Freud, the father of psychiatry, or if he did, he did not quite understand him. Listening—and sometimes listening endlessly—in the hope of discovering a connection is the essence both of psychiatry and pastoral counseling.[3]

Christina Puchalski, M.D., is another one of the many recently emerging experts in pastoral care and counseling, the vast majority of which are theologically and psychoanalytically unschooled. She rides the spirituality horse to its limit. It all sounds so good to uninformed lay people. But no one quite knows what she means when she so often invokes the sacred category "spirituality." Perhaps it refers to anything one wishes it to mean. Spirituality is suggestive of religion, but of course, as the au courant saying goes, one can be spiritual without being religious, which sounds very much like saying "religious but not religious."

Thus the spirituality gang has the burden of producing some credible definitions. In ancient history spirituality did have meaning, suggesting a life force rooted in breathing. But we cannot use words today as if they mean what they meant on the streets of Athens or Jerusalem two or three thousand years ago. Etymology does not permit that. Many theologians have cautioned that "spirituality" is a lost word, detached from an earlier powerful set of meanings, but only fools go on using it today as if it still means what it used to mean. That's Puchalski. She may as well be speaking Portuguese to the English-speaking world.

And then there is Herbert Benson, M.D., yet another marquee nontheologian, who seeks to demonstrate that a hundred people praying for the same patient produces more effective results than one person doing the same praying. Benson's claim to fame could be said to be that he is the father of "the commodification of prayer" initiative. As in, if you have one hundred outlet stores you will be richer than having just one outlet store. Benson was given a $2.4 million grant by the John Templeton Foundation in 1998 with the commission to prove his case that the more people we have praying for the same patient the better will be the health results of that patient: positivism run rampant. With a big bag of money Benson produced what became known as "The Great Prayer Experiment," officially "The Study of the Therapeutic Effects of Intercessory Prayer" (STEP). The study involved 1800 coronary artery bypass surgery patients in six hospitals, and three Christian congregations doing the praying, having been provided only the patients' first names and the initials of their surnames. The design established a control group of one-third of the patients who were not prayed for. The remaining two-thirds were divided into two groups, one group being told they were being prayed for and the other being told that they may or may not be prayed for. Benson set out to prove that those who were prayed for would show higher survival rates. Along with a lot of other people, I could have told Benson in advance, for a fee of much less than $2.4 million, that his clinical trial was not going to produce what he wanted it to produce. Prayers do not commodify. The delicious part of the results of The Great Prayer Study was that the patients in the control group who had no prayers said on their behalf did marginally better than the other groups who were prayed for by hundreds, including a trainload of nuns.

Perhaps it is irreverent to wonder who got their hands on the bulk of that $2.4 million. I doubt it was the nuns.

The latest star in the efforts to commodify prayer and spirituality is the sociologist, Wendy Cadge. Like Koenig, Benson, and Puchalski, she too is theologically untrained, and it shows. In 2012, Cadge published *Paging God: Religion in the Halls of Medicine*. If ever there was an inept metaphor for the work of a chaplain, paging god would arguably be at the top of the list. A god who is available on demand is no god at all. And a chaplain who is presumed to have power to page a god as he would an errand boy would justly be murdered on the streets as a danger to humanity. The real problem with Cadge, Benson, Puchalski, Koenig, and many others of like mind is that they are functioning outside their area of expertise.

Unlike any attempt to be spiritual, we do know more or less what it means to be pastoral. To be pastoral is to function like a shepherd or farmer caring for the life and welfare of the flock and the land. That is a specific and concrete task. A shepherd concerns herself with the life and welfare of all her animal and plant life, and the earth itself. As the military likes to say, shepherding is "boots on the ground." When the flock is in danger or the crop is at risk, the shepherd knows what to do. We can understand what shepherding or pastoring means. In addition to the concept of pastoral, we also know clearly what counseling and psychotherapy mean: listening to a troubled person. And that means sometimes endlessly listening, until a pattern emerges or connections reveal themselves that might lead to clarity and a deeper understanding of the exigencies of life.

Now, close to a century after Boisen inaugurated the clinical pastoral movement, the picture is mixed and contradictory. On the one hand, the place of clinically trained religious professionals in clinical settings seems to have been greatly strengthened by an increase in numbers. On the other hand, there is an inchoate sense abroad that pastoral clinicians lack direction and a clear sense of what the task is. This is a very dark shadow on the future.

The late Donald Capps, in a private communication with me, made an observation that is pertinent in this context. He said: "Any encounter between a religious authority and a patient or parishioner is ipso facto religious, just as any consultation between patient and physician is ipso facto medical." The implied authority of the office ensures that. Nothing specific need occur in either instance. The encounter does not require prayer or any discussion of spirituality, however defined. The agreement between the religious authority and the subject to converse is itself the outcome, or the first of perhaps many outcomes. Nothing need be added, neither prayer, nor sacrament, nor discussion of spirituality. Regardless of what is done or said, or left undone or unsaid, the encounter is by definition pastoral and religious. Sometimes the pastor, and sometimes the physician, essentially does nothing. Or perhaps they simply listen, as Oates describes doing in the above Prologue. Following Capps' observation, the current urgency of institutional chaplains to pray with patients, an impulse quite widespread, suggests that chaplains are anxious, lacking in confidence about their inherent role as religious authorities and the aura that is carried with that role.

In the same way, the physician is never required to provide any specific information, or to perform any specific procedure at any given time, or to provide any specific test when approached by a patient. So it is also with the pastor.

30.
A PERSONAL DETOUR

I had occasion in the spring of 2016 to visit my friend and one-time clinical pastoral supervisor, a mentor from my younger years, Chappell Wilson. He is a widower now, living in a retirement community in the Atlanta area, and very comfortable there. The visit was something of a culture shock. I was reminded in spending the day with Chappell, of the saying, almost a motto, of prisoners I used to work with in the Houston jail: "What goes around comes around." Both Chappell and I lived through the early years of the Sexual Revolution. I was in training with him just as it began to flower in earnest. I was not a hippie (too old for that), but I was a fellow traveler and did have a large flower pasted on the door of my Volkswagen. In Chappell's retirement community, the Sexual Revolution "has gone around and come around."

We both worked in institutional chaplaincy in the later years when the strife and enmity of the sexual counterrevolution began to be felt. These were very difficult years in the relationships between men and women, particularly in the clinical pastoral arena. The gender war was just warming up. It would get much worse.

Chappell's retirement community is a very quiet, comfortable, and well-appointed place. It is a world mostly of women, and they clearly suffer from a paucity of men. The health of men fails earlier, in general, and they typically die earlier than women.

As I entered the facility as a guest, it became clear to me that some of the women seemed to think that I might be an incoming resident. After all, I am older than Chappell. I believe it was with that prospect I received an exceedingly warm welcome. I noticed that all eyes were on me, in a manner of speaking. The scarcity of males seemed to be experienced by the women residents as a great loss. I felt a strong, mostly unspoken invitation to "come live with us." After decades of life under the baleful weight of the sexual counterrevolution, where every male was seen first as an incipient sexual predator, this was a shocking reversal. As an adult male, I was suddenly dropped into a mostly female community and welcomed, as it were, with open arms. What a shock that was after enduring so much of "women supervising women."

Attending the afternoon musicale where there was a mere scattering of men, mostly feeble, I was struck by the hungry eyes of the numerous women, many fixed on me. There was some dancing, but it was mostly women dancing with women. I danced with a couple of grateful and charming women, and with pleasure.

Chappell shared with me candidly what life there was like. He finds it quite comfortable. But the women—or at least the heterosexual ones—are mostly deprived sexually and suffering because of it. Sexual relationships are scarce, but highly sought after by healthy women. The few males have their pick and can be choosy, and need not follow monogamous rules. Marriage and exclusive commitments are generally irrelevant and seemingly of no currency for most in that setting, or so I was told. In a real sense, it seemed to me a blessed community where persons are free to do as they please sexually, with no harsh moralistic judgments coming down on them for finding any meager sexual gratification they can find. Sexual overtures are not referred to as "hits," as in "hit on," the current lingo in the wider culture levied against a male who makes even a subtle overture toward a woman. There was no evidence of the sex police in action, assessments that Chappell confirmed.

After my visit with Chappell I thought I might say to any younger woman who is offended because some stray male "hit on" her, that the days will come, if she lives so long, when she will view such hits through a different prism, not necessarily as aggressive assaults but more as invitations to dance. And because men die younger, I might say to that woman, the day may come when she will recall such invitations with great fondness and wistfulness, and indubitably regret that they are now few and far between, if they occur at all.

The experience and decision of retired Supreme Court Justice Sandra Day O'Connor is congruent with my experience of Chappell Wilson's retirement community. O'Connor placed her husband in a retirement facility because of her inability to cope with his progressing Alzheimer's disease. He soon paired with a female resident in a sexual relationship, and O'Conner readily gave her blessing to these geriatric lovebirds, even though they were technically adulterers. She could have responded differently had she been a conventional American woman. Had O'Connor responded in typical fashion, she would have portrayed herself as a wronged woman or attacked her husband for playing the predatory male role. She was too wise and too cultured for that.

My visit with Chappell Wilson showed me that old age is perhaps the price we all may have to pay for both sexual wisdom and sexual freedom. And this is the kind of sexual wisdom that was demonstrated by many of the leading figures of the clinical pastoral movement over the past century. Some of them, blessedly, found wisdom and freedom prior to their retirement years and prior to the onslaught of the sexual counter-revolution.

My visit to Chappell was comparable to seeing a fulfillment of Isaiah: the lion and the lamb lying down together.

31.
LAST WORDS

"Sexual love is undoubtedly one of the chief things in life. The union of mental and bodily satisfaction in the enjoyment of love is one of its culminating peaks. Apart from a few queer fanatics, all the world knows this and conducts its life accordingly; science alone is too delicate to admit it."
— Sigmund Freud [4]

Any reader might be puzzled by the recurring centrality of sexual issues in the history of the century-old clinical pastoral movement. Some readers may even be tempted to discard this entire account of mine on grounds that it is sex-obsessed. The rejoinder must be that sex is a universal problem that is often kept under wraps or out of awareness. The clinical pastoral movement, like Sigmund Freud, simply brought the issue out of the closet and into the light of day, at least in its early decades. It is not much of a stretch to say that human beings in general are simply consciously or unconsciously sex-obsessed. What to do with sexual desire in ourselves and in others is a question that has no final resolution anywhere with anyone who loves and affirms life. Sexuality is the one aspect of human existence that consistently defies rational oversight and control. At best we are all works in progress on this matter.

And lest someone charge the clinical pastoral movement with being uniquely obsessed about sexuality, we should remember that Christianity itself—just to name one world religion that is closest to our experience—is a history of massive attention to sexual issues, both for good and for ill, and mostly for the latter. No other issue in the human experience has engaged the attention of Christian authorities through the centuries like sexuality. The later history of Christianity, after the fourth century, is a history of celibacy, monastic life, separation of genders, and at once, the promotion of and simultaneous repression of homosexuality. Christianity from about the fourth century onward has taken an extreme position in prohibiting sexual pleasure except under the most limited circumstances, for purposes of procreation. Among world religions Christianity is the most obsessively masochistic as regards sexual pleasure. Even in our relatively enlightened era we remain under that cloud. No one who identifies as a Christian will have any standing to accuse the clinical pastoral movement of being obsessed with sex. In 1944, in the midst of the final throes of the Nazi holocaust, Pope Pius XII found time and energy to convene a meeting of church leaders in order to address the evil of extramarital sex. He was clearly more vexed by the many Italian women being deflowered by Allied soldiers than he was of the six million persons being exterminated in Central Europe.[5]

Therefore, let it be said loud and clear, that the clinical pastoral movement is not an outlier in its peculiar helter-skelter history of attempting to sort out virtue from vice in the sexual arena. The movement has simply been more candid and honest about sexual behavior. Anton Boisen is not an historical freak in his painful and eminently unsuccessful struggle to integrate sexual pleasure into his life and remain obedient to what he believed was commanded of him by his religion. His uniqueness was simply that he endured several psychotic breaks, and yet, in spite of that, remained extraordinarily faithful, creative, and useful to society—a remarkable achievement.

The century-long clinical pastoral movement sparked by Anton Boisen was and continues to be a long struggle to implement ethical and effective therapeutic approaches for working with suffering people, particularly those suffering mostly in their minds. Boisen himself learned from reading Freud, while in psychiatric lockup, that a disordered mind, at least in some cases, was the result of a struggle to find integration in the face of powerful internal conflicts. He knew that to be the case for himself. And like so many, he was aware that his internal conflicts were rooted in his own sexual desire as it collided with his wish to be religiously faithful.

During his psychiatric lockup, Boisen became persuaded by and committed to Freud's talking cure. "All I do is listen and make connections," wrote Freud. This was the psychoanalytic method. And Freud never lost faith in it. Boisen took this as an injunction. He followed Freud in this approach as he worked with disturbed and psychotic persons. And needless to say, one need not be psychotic to suffer mentally. On this premise and vision Boisen founded the clinical pastoral movement in 1925.

In Boisen's own case this struggle and search for integration began with his violent and threatening—as he experienced it—circumcision at age four, when his mother found him pleasuring himself sexually. He introjected this negative message for the rest of his life. The sudden inopportune death from a coronary of his sexually promiscuous father at age 38, when Boisen was seven, likely reinforced the message of sexual prohibition. After four decades of wandering in his lostness, Boisen discovered the possibility of therapy by way of the talking cure, which would be better labeled "the listening cure," through his reading of Freud.

Boisen then proposed that pastors make use of Freud's talking cure as more effective than their talking, preaching, and praying. That Boisen never seemed to have found someone to listen to him must remain a puzzle and a point of terrible irony. In spite of the poverty in his own sensual life, Boisen founded a monumental movement. His alliance with the genius psychiatrist and theologian, Helen Flanders Dunbar, resulted in a grand alliance with the nation's Protestant seminaries in the decade of the 1930s, which resulted in the golden age of the clinical pastoral movement.

After about 15 years the movement spawned by Boisen began to become uncomfortable with Freud. His links with sex began to fray nerves and frighten the natives. Then in 1940, Wilhelm Reich came to the U.S. Fright turned to panic. Soon any pastoral clinician following Reich's approach was threatened with loss of credentials among pastoral clinicians. What followed was a gradual separation from a psychoanalytic approach in all respects. The baby was beginning to be thrown out with the bath water. In the 1960s, the Sexual Revolution emerged, bringing more anxiety. This was followed in the latter two decades of the century with women's liberation, their anger, and their perfectly understandable though ultimately destructive grasping for immediate power and their antipathy toward men.

The distancing of the clinical pastoral movement from its creative origins was concurrent with the disempowerment of Boisen and Dunbar personally. The dynamic alliance of clinical pastoral training and psychoanalytic thought began to unravel ever so gradually. Clinical pastoral training lost its direction and eventually its soul. Didacticism filled the vacuum.

The monumental missed opportunity of the century was the chance for pastoral clinicians to link up explicitly with Freud's theories in a united effort toward addressing mental suffering, not simply for the certifiably insane, but also for relatively normal persons who were troubled over their decisions, their thought processes, their dreams, and the exigencies of life.

Freud himself seems to have made overtures to the religious community. In fact, he may have done everything short of getting baptized in his invitation to Christians to make an alliance with him. One could say that Freud had an unrequited love for the best of religious work. While he was dismissive of orthodox Christian organization and theology, he was happy to train ministers as lay analysts, the Swiss Lutheran pastor, the Rev. Oscar Pfister, being a notable example.

In Freud's view a minister could be a competent analyst. There was no need for medical training and no need to be a physician. Freud contended that the great mass of what is taught in medical school is of no use to the analyst. "Psychoanalysis is not a specialized branch of medicine," he wrote. Much of what is required to be taught in medical school is of little or no use to a psychoanalyst. A competent analyst needs only to know the history of civilization, mythology, the psychology of religion, and significant world literature, he wrote. "Unless he is well at home in these subjects, an analyst can make nothing of a large amount of his material."[6]

Freud wrote *The Question of Lay Analysis* in 1926, in response to the Vienna Psychoanalytical Society's attempt to prevent nonmedical persons from practicing psychoanalysis. In 1927 he added an exclamation mark with a brief explicit postscript. This work is stunningly concurrent, both chronologically and philosophically, with Boisen's inauguration of clinical pastoral training, which was founded on Freud's own constructs. Freud wrote that after 41 years of medical activity, "my self-knowledge tells me that I have never been a doctor in the proper sense."[7] He even surmised that physicians aimed to take possession of psychoanalysis for the purpose of destroying it. If he could return from the dead he would likely say today that his fears came to fruition.[8]

> "My innate sadistic disposition was not a very strong one, so that I had no need to develop this one of its derivatives. Nor did I ever play the doctor game.... In my youth I felt an overpowering need to understand something of the riddles of the world."

Freud looked longingly at both clergy and social workers as potential followers, to carry forward his vision of lay analysis. They were the most promising disciplines that might have supplanted medicine as the organizational vehicle for psychoanalysis.[9]

> "Perhaps once more an American may hit on the idea of spending a little money to get the social workers of his country trained analytically and to turn them into a band of helpers for combating the neurosis of civilization."

He continued piquantly,[10]

> "Aha! A new kind of Salvation Army! And if so, this new army will have to bypass Vienna where lay analysis has succumbed to a premature trauma of prohibition."

Freud's implicit rapprochement with clergy is revealed in the language he used to describe his own functioning. He wrote that the label "secular pastoral worker" might serve as a general formula for describing the function that the analyst, whether he is a doctor or a layman, has to perform in relation to the public.[11]

A great loss to civilization is that Freud, the consummate *secular pastoral worker,* who brought an offer of salvation, that is, healing, was unable to motivate more than a few religious pastoral workers. And those few were mostly the followers of Boisen. It is doubtful that Freud's self-acknowledged atheism was the inhibiting factor here. Surely the real block to a joint effort was the incipient panic among the religious population over Freud's candid observations about sex. Christians in particular fear sex more than any other aspect of the human experience, or even the devil himself.

While Freud as an atheist was not interested in promoting religious work as such, he was committed to pastoring suffering persons from his secular perch. In that respect he was a natural ally to all seriously religious persons who also seek to assist suffering persons. Boisen was one of the few who understood that. As Freud put it,[12]

> "We who are analysts do not seek to bring the patient relief by receiving him into the Catholic, Protestant, or socialist community. We seek rather to enrich him from his own internal sources, by putting at the disposal of his ego those energies which, owing to repression, are inaccessibly confined in his unconscious, as well as those which his ego is obliged to squander in the fruitless task of maintaining these repressions. Such activity as this is *pastoral work* in the best sense of the words."... and "it is only by carrying on our *analytic pastoral work* that we can deepen our dawning comprehension of the human mind." [italics mine]

However, there was a missing piece in Freud's vision of pastoring that the religiously oriented could remedy. Freud had no vision of community. As a physician, that vision would not have come naturally to him. He was very much a loner. The religious tradition generally aspires to bring people together in a flock, assembly, or congregation—or chapter—for mutual sustenance. Freud's citing of pastoral lacked the fullness of the shepherding dimension, as in creating and caring for a group and its continuity. Seward Hiltner had earlier argued, correctly, that healing and shepherding could not be separated. As a typical physician, Freud focused on particular individuals and seemingly had no vision of a continuing healing community. Thus, while Freud taught the religious community about the unconscious and the necessity of exploring one's personal history in the service of healing, the religious community might have taught Freud about the therapeutic effect of a sustaining and continuing community, also in the service of healing. But it was not to be. Freud's invitation may have been too tentative, but the Christian culture's fear of sexuality would, in any case, almost certainly have trumped any overt initiative from Freud.

As the new century unfolded in 2001, women were generally angry and in control in the clinical pastoral movement, and males were generally confused and inhibited. The role of the pastoral clinician had become blurred, bereft of definition. Into this vacuum marched a number of physicians and psychologists who posed as amateur theologians and redefined the pastoral task as one of summoning the powers of the gods for the benefit of suffering persons. The relative success of this incursion wrote fini on any notion that pastoral clinicians were actually clinicians any longer. They became pastoral fantasists under the suasion of these new amateur religious leaders with their grab bags of spirituality.

In such dire straits the only conceivable hope now is for pastoral clinicians to stage a resurrection, or insurrection, and reassert the Freud-Boisen-Dunbar thesis. That thesis asserts that healing comes when an intelligent and informed pastoral person listens carefully and mostly silently to the accounts of a suffering person. And in that listening always keeping the unconscious and its perverse and unpredictable ways clearly in view—at least in the corner of the eye—and observing whatever connections can be made that might promote healing. Which is to say, the only hope for the future for pastoral clinicians lies in a reassertion of the authentic talking cure that was promoted by Anton Boisen and Helen Flanders Dunbar, a cure they learned from Sigmund Freud. And we must add, supplemented by attention to community building, a calling in which religious communities have historically demonstrated some expertise.

Boisen's vision was that all religious professionals be clinically trained. He desired no new profession of pastoral psychologists. Every pastor should be a psychoanalytically informed pastoral clinician, in Boisen's view. In his own words Boisen wrote, "I shall assume that counseling is the nonmedical term for psychotherapy."[13] Through the decades many pastoral clinicians, Robert Brinkman being the most notable example, separated from their religious identity and became independent psychotherapists. That may have been a viable choice for some, and it may have been the only viable choice for Brinkman and others like him, but that shift was not part of Boisen's vision. He sought to make every religious leader psychologically competent to help suffering persons. And for him, psychologically competent meant psychoanalytically competent. Had Freud seen the Boisen movement coming, he would have been deeply gratified. Boisen's vision was congruent with Freud's own vision of an emerging great army of lay psychoanalysts.

Boisen's life was shipwrecked on the treacherous shoals of sexual pleasure. He never found enough therapy for himself to reconstruct his own personal life. He seems to have lived for 89 years bereft of sexual pleasure of any sort, and beyond that, a bit suspicious of any signs of a liberated sexuality in others. However, in his acquisition of Freud's talking cure he knew he had found what every troubled soul needed, an intelligent, informed, therapeutic listener. Though he never seems to have found that kind of healing for himself, he set out to train other ministers to be that kind of therapeutic listener. He created a movement that by mid-century changed the character of American religion, the clinical pastoral movement. But history does not move upwards on an inclined plane. It moves through action and counteraction. By the end of the century, the clinical pastoral movement had for the most part repudiated Boisen, Dunbar, and Freud, and itself had become shipwrecked on the same treacherous shoals of sexual pleasure that had undone Boisen personally.

From the wreckage of Boisen's life, as well as from his greatness, and from the wreckage of the clinical pastoral movement as well as its glories, future generations now have at least the knowledge and tools to create a better future for anyone who is willing.

APPENDIX

Letters from Wayne Oates to Raymond Lawrence

January 9, 1994

Dear Raymond Lawrence,

Thank you from the heart for your thoughtful letter and your book. I have already read well into the book, *The Poisoning of Eros* and now can hardly put it down until I have finished it. Your research is in the primary sources and not pop psychology, and your perception of sexuality makes more sense than anything I have read. I will be recommending it to many people. I will not lend it. It is mine! Thank you!

I am grateful for your reading my *Struggle to Be Free*. I wrote it ten years ago and each year since then has validated my emphasis in the book. And after reading your letter I felt a strong congruence with you. As I finish your book, I will write you again, but at this time I want to express my gratitude to you.

Your comments about my days with the CCT bring back many memories. I greatly appreciate your sending me the Covenant of CPSP. I myself have not supervised any ACPE students since 1988. The certification process chews up some very good people and I continue hear horror stories about it. The money, property, power and prestige concerns of the bureaucracy take otherwise decent people and put them to work at cold and arrogant tasks. It is time someone does something about it. You seem to be creating a fellowship and not another bureaucracy.

Dr. Boisen told me on one occasion that his dream was for a fellowship and not a certifying and approving people, that people of a common concern about people in need and commitment to the clinical approach should all be welcome.

When the Committee of Twelve met in the early fifties to hammer out agreed-upon standards of clinical pastoral care, we functioned as a fellowship for years until a super-organization was formed in 1967.

Now to get behind an Associate Supervisor's status is a tortuous repetition of rejections instead of fulfillment.

Dr. Boisen was a research man as is evident you are. But to do research and publish it is alien to the CPE process.

Keep up the good work of being a fellowship and being the kind of research person your book shows you to be.

Myron Madden, Chappell Wilson - good friends over the decades!

Gratefully yours,

Wayne Oates

•••

January 22, 1994

Dear Raymond Lawrence,

I have read your book, *The Poisoning of Eros* line for line all the way through and I am indebted to you for the journey we travelled together.

In the first place, I was grateful for the careful handling of primary sources, many of them hard to find, all the way through the book. You unearthed sources I had never heard of and I am greatly edified by your hard work.

In the second place, with a college major in philosophy, I was firmly schooled in the stark dualism of the Greco-Roman sources, particularly Plato. Aquinas is severely in debt to Aristotle. The mishandling of the Hebrew appreciation of the unity of personality that makes sex good and vigorous is set aside by the Platonic view.

In the third place, I am deeply grateful for your handling of Barth and Tillich's personal sexual histories. I knew Tillich personally when he was at Union. I have been with him in the company of women. They were sensually drawn to him. They felt what seemed to be an aura of communion with him. He and Hannah had a distinctly continental ethic of sex not unakin to O'Neill and O'Neill's *Open Marriage*.

One of the things I think contributed to such negatives as may be in the O.T. and N.T. towards sex is the problem of promiscuity. This raises the issue of sexually transmitted diseases and unwanted pregnancies. This was implicit but not explicit in your treatise. Then, too, in this day of sexual harassment when schoolteachers are urged not to hug a child that wants to hug them, I wonder if we are not moving into a strange Puritanism.

Your book is a most serious discussion of sexuality, far more substantive than anything I have read. It reminded me of an older book by David Mace, *Hebrew Marriage*. If you can locate it, I think you will find an intellectual kinsperson.

With much gratitude to you, my newfound friend, I am

Faithfully yours,

Wayne

•••

January 26, 1994

Dear Raymond,

Thank you for your good letter. It is an inspiration to me to know about the availability of your book, *The Poisoning of Eros*. One reason for the silence of professors is that they probably did not take the time to read it. If they had, they would have been informed by your intensive use of primary sources and by the forcefulness of your vision of church history from another angle of vision - sexuality. The privatization of sexuality is rampant in theological schools. For example, at Southern Baptist Seminary, we have a handbook of policies of the school. On sexual matters, six lines are devoted to sexual behavior. Three pages are devoted to parking rules!

Thank you for the excellent review of Harold Bloom's book. I am acquainted with his work. I bought and read his *The Book of J* which gives a much more realistic approach to that part of the O.T. than commentaries do.

I am eager to get his book on *American Religion*. He is right about the overwhelming majority of Southern Baptists being gnostic, especially about sexuality. This concern is almost identical with Roman Catholicism: anti-contraception, anti-sex for the enjoyment and not merely for procreation, anti-abortions for any reason, etc.

However, I think there is a social class factor in this. Those of us born and raised in the lower classes tend to have a much more realistic view of sexuality, for example, such things as living together, pre-marital sexuality, and reverence for a child born out of wedlock have been for decades commonplace among the poor.

The Gnostics are middle class in origin and present attitude. The same thing about sexuality also applies to the expression of anger. For example, in CPE, the emphasis is on "getting in touch with your anger." This is a middle-class concern. The person from a poverty background is trying to get over using his fists to settle arguments!

I had memorized E.Y. Mullins when I was a student. He does place the emphasis on subjective experience. However, he was heavily influenced by William James' *Varieties of Religious Experience*. On the ground that he covered, I was able with the help of four senior faculty members to introduce students at the Seminary here to depth psychology in the psychology of religion.

I very much appreciate your sending me your review of *American Religion*. I am confident that one of the reasons for the psychotherapeutic slant of preaching today is the background of

Gnostic thinking among American Christians. Yet churches are unwilling to support counselors on their staff. They say as one Board of Deacons did: "That is for mentally disturbed people and we don't have anybody like that in our church!"

Thank you again, Raymond!

Faithfully yours,

Wayne

•••

November 27, 1996

Dear Raymond,

Thank you for your letter, your invitation, and the copies of *Contra Mundum*. I wish I could accept your invitation to be a consultant at the Plenary meeting of the College of Pastoral Supervision and Psychotherapy. The format is exciting and I wish I could be there.

My reason for not being there is a constant, chronic pain syndrome due to six bad discs in my spine and an unstable left leg due to a C-6 C-7 involvement that did not respond adequately to surgery. I can do my work around here but I cannot travel.

You are certainly right in placing certification in the hands of people who know them personally and have seen their work over a period of time. The committees and the bureaucracy are too costly, often wound people unnecessarily and drive other applicants away.

Thank you again for your generous invitation.

Faithfully yours,

Wayne

•••

June 13, 1999

Dear Raymond,

Thank you for your letter of condolence about the death of our son, Bill. He was a Vietnam combat veteran and died after a severe head injury from a fall. He lived a life tortured by PTSD and its flashbacks from the war. We are broken-hearted but will live a day at a time and thank God for it. We thank God that Bill is with him and at peace.

You are right. I am not traveling now. I have several disc problems in my spine and stenosis of the spinal cord that makes my balance and walk unstable. So I don't travel anymore. I would love to be at your CPSP but for this.

Faithfully yours,

Wayne

ENDNOTES

Epigraph

¹ "The Minister and Psychotherapy," *Pastoral Psychology*, Feb. 1960, p. 11, cited by Edward E. Thornton, *Professional Education for Ministry: A History of Clinical Pastoral Education*, Nashville: Abington Press, 1970. p. 236

Preface

² Karl Barth, *Ethics*, Dietrich Brown, ed., Geoffrey W. Bromiley, trans., New York: The Seabury Press, 1981, p. 187ff.

Prologue

¹ Thornton, *op.cit.*, p. 153ff.

² Sigmund Freud, *Collected Papers*, vol. 4, p. 212

Chapter 1 — Boisen

¹ Anton T. Boisen, *Exploration of the Inner World: A Study of Mental Disorder and Religious Experience*, New York: 1936, p. 239.

² See John Money, *The Destroying Angel: Sex, Fitness and Food in the Legacy of Degeneracy Theory*, Prometheus Books, 1985.

³ Elizabeth Roudinesco, *Freud in His Time and Ours*, Catharine Porter, trans., Harvard University Press, 2016, p. 76

⁴ Personal letters of Boisen, housed at Chicago Theological Seminary, and collected by David Roth, with the generous assistance of the former archivist-librarian, Evan Boyd.

⁵ Seward Hiltner, "Fifty Years of CPE," *Journal of Pastoral Care*, 29:2, June 1, 1975, pp. 90-98.

⁶ Paul W. Pruyser, "Anton Boisen and the Psychology of Religion," pp. 145-56, in *Vision from a Little Known Country: A Boisen Reader*, Glen H. Asquith Jr, Ed.

⁷ Boisen, *op.cit, Exploration...*, p. 101

⁸ Paul E. Johnson, "Fifty Years of Clinical Pastoral Education," presented to Meyer Memorial Hospital, Buffalo, NY, June 28, 1967. Later published in *Journal of Pastoral Care*.

⁹ Personal letters of Boisen, housed at Chicago Theological Seminary.

¹⁰ Document held in Henri J. M. Nouwen Archives and Research Collection, University of Toronto: nouwen.archives@utoronto.ca

¹¹ Personal communication, L. George Buck.

¹² Phone interview with Clarence Bruninga, March 9, 2000. Bruninga was Boisen's trainee in 1951-52, and on staff with him 1953-1963. He said that it was a struggle working with Boisen, that he became inflexible, and that "he did a good job of offending everyone who worked with him."

¹³ Charles E. Hall, *Head and Heart: The Story of the Clinical Pastoral Education Movement*, Journal of Pastoral Care Publications Inc., 1992, p. 11.

¹⁴ Hall, *op.cit.*, p. 11; also from Hiltner, "The Heritage of Anton T. Boisen," *Pastoral Psychology*, Vol. 16, No. 158.

¹⁵ Hall, *Ibid*, p.11-12

¹⁶ Richard J. Lehman. "Some Footnotes on a Glorious Tradition," unpublished and undated paper, circulated by author after March 4, 2004.

¹⁷ Allison Stokes, *Ministry After Freud*, New York: The Pilgrim Press, 1985, p. 71.

Chapter 2 — Helen Flanders Dunbar

¹ Robert Charles Powell, Anton T. Boisen: Breaking an Opening in The Wall Between Religion and Medicine, published by the Association of Mental Health Clergy, 1976, p. 16. This is the most incise in-depth description of Boisen's work and contribution known to me.

² Edward Thornton, *op.cit.*, gives the address of 730 Park Avenue. This is now a 20-story, luxury apartment building that was built in 1928. Today apartments sell there for $20 million and up. Robert Charles Powell, in a personal communication with Dunbar's daughter, Marcia Dunbar-Soule Dobson, remembers that in the 1940's they lived at 3 East 69th St., and that both office and apartment were on the first

floor, She took an office next to the alley between two buildings opposite each other. Later they moved to a new building next door, at 1 East 69th Street. She later bought an apartment at 1 East 66th Street. She also had an office and apartment, and later a home, in Greenwich, CT.

[3] Thornton, *op.cit.*, pp. 87-8.

[4] *Ibid*, pp. 96ff.

Chapter 3 — The Emergence of Seward Hiltner

[5] Porter French, "Innocents Abroad: Clinical Pastoral Education in the Early Days," *Journal of Pastoral Care*, 29:1, March 1975, pp. 7-10.

[6] Hiltner in "Fifty Years of CPE," *op.cit.*, p. 92.

[7] Hiltner, *Ibid*, p. 97-8.

Chapter 4 — The Legacy of Russell L. Dicks

[8] E. Brooks Holifield, *A History of Pastoral Care in America: From Salvation to Self-Realization*, Eugene, OR, Wipf & Stock, 1983, p. 242. It should be noted that Holifield did not really understand Boisen, characterizing him as focused on self-realization.

[9] S.A.Lewis, M.D., and John Gilmore, Ph.D, *Sex after Forty: The Book of Hope for Men and Women in or Nearing the Turbulent Years*, "Introduction" by The Reverend Dr. Russell L. Dicks, Professor of Pastoral Care, Duke University, Medical Research Press, 1952, p. 9.

[10] *Ibid.*

[11] *Ibid.*

Chapter 5 — The First Quarter Century

[12] Roudinesco, *op.cit.*, pp. 37-8

[13] p. 18ff, for polygamy in Jewish history, Raymond J. Lawrence, *The Poisoning of Eros: Sexual Values in Conflict*, Augustine Moore Press, 1989.
Louis Menard, in "The Stone Guest: Can Sigmund Freud ever be killed?", *The New Yorker*, August 28, 2017, pp. 75-82, assesses the current unrelenting assault on Freud. He reviews the work of the Freud bashers, Peter Swales, Jeffrey Moussaieff

Masson, and Frederick Crews who have gone all out to prove that Freud was some kind of dangerous psychopath. One of their major charges in trashing Freud is the conjecture that Freud was sexually involved with Minna. In light of Jewish religious history Freud's alleged sexual relationship with his sister-in-law, in the context of an otherwise abstemious life, does nothing at all to impugn Freud's honor except in the eyes of the bourgeois Christian right.

[14] Lehman, *op.cit.*

[15] *Ibid.*

[16] Reuel Howe, "The Role of Clinical Training in Theological Education," *Journal of Pastoral Care*, 1952, pp. 5-6.

[17] Thornton, *op.cit.*, p. 96
[In June 1944, gathering of all groups, Hiltner commented in his conclusion to the published proceedings: [p107 Thornton]
"...[This] is the first conference on clinical training...which has brought honest disagreements into the open and yet has avoided acrimony...there has been no attempt... to suggest that complete uniformity or organic union be achieved now or in any foreseeable future within the clinical training movement. Yet there has been agreement that cooperative relationships must be maintained now that they have been established, and that there needs to be representative group conferring together on additional specific point at which cooperation is possible."

Chapter 6 — The Tower of Babel Redux

[19] Thornton, *op.cit.*, p. 92.

[20] Hall, op.cit., p. 67

[21] Ibid, p. 63; Thornton, op.cit., p. 123.

Chapter 7 — Wilhelm Reich: The Orgone and Pastoral Counselors

[22] Freud to Andreas-Salome, July 28, 1929, in Sigmund Freud and Lou Andreas-Salome, *Letters*, ed. Ernst Pfeiffer, trans. William Robson-Scott and Elaine Robson-Scott, New York: Harcourt Brace Jovanovich, 1972, pp. 181-82, and Roudinesco, *op.cit.*, p. 340.

Chapter 8 — Speaking with One Voice: The Creation of The ACPE

[23] Hall, *op.cit.*, pp. 125-6.

[24] Ibid, p. 135.

[25] *Ibid*, p. 141.

[26] *Ibid*, pp. 100, 159.

[27] *Ibid*, p. 149.

Chapter 13 — Joan E. Hemenway

[28] *The Journal of Religion and Health*, Vol. 36, No. 1, March 1997, pp. 91-3.

Chapter 17 — Cigarettes, Whiskey, Women and Poker

[29] Hall, *op.cit.*, p. 96

[30] Spring, 1989

Chapter 20 — The Creation of The College of Pastoral Supervision and Psychotherapy

[31] At the Houston meeting an informal group gathered twice to discuss the matter of founding an alternate organization. Finally there was a consensus to do so. No one present argued against taking this action. Those present who finally authorized the initiative were Ben Breitkreuz, Bill Carr, Jim Daugherty, Wayland Johnson, Gwinnett Grier, Howard Hanchey, Janet Lutz, Bob Pierce, Jeffrey Silberman, Ray Stephens, Ted Trout-Landen, David Wyatt, and Raymond Lawrence.

[32] The CPSP organizing group in Roanoke consisted of Al Anderson, Julian Byrd (who abstained), Bill Carr, Bob Clayton, Richard Dayringer, Gwynette Grier, Don Gum, Wayland Johnson, Raymond Lawrence, Janet Lutz, Pat McCoy, Jarvis McMillan, Perry Miller, David Moss, Ray Stephens, and Chappell Wilson. Absent but communicating in writing an interest were Eugene Allen, Ed Babinsky, Richard Blice, Pres Borgia, Serge Castigliano, Jim Dougherty, Alan Hanson, Cathy Hasty, Peter Keene, John Mackey, Carol Nash, Pat Prest, Henry Taxis, Jack Stearns, Nick Ristad, and Bob Lantz.

Chapter 29 — Now At This Juncture

[1] Which was then referred to as "The Joint Commission on Accreditation of Healthcare Organizations," or "JCAHO," a non-governmental organization that provides public credibility to health care institutions for a fee.

[2] George Fitchett & Steve Nolan, eds., *Spiritual Care in Practice: Case Studies in Healthcare Chaplaincy*, Foreword by Christian M. Puchalski, Afterword by John Swindon, Philadelphia: Jessica Kingsley Publishers, 2015. For a Critique of Fitchett and Nolan, see Raymond J. Lawrence, *Nine Clinical Cases: The Soul of Pastoral Care and Counseling*, 2015.

[3] Harold Koenig, "An 84-Year-Old Woman With Chronic Illness and Strong Religious Beliefs", *Journal of the American Medical Association*, June 14, 2002. Commented on in "Vicissitudes of Spirituality," Raymond J. Lawrence, pp. 105-121, in *The Healing Power of Spirituality: How Faith Helps Humans Thrive, Volume 1, Personal Spirituality*, J. Harold Ellens, Ed., Praeger ABC-CLIO, 2010.

Chapter 31 — Last Words

[4] Sigmund Freud, "Observations on Transference Love," 1915.

[5] Address of Pope Pius XII to the Italian Medical-Biological Union of St. Luke, Nov. 12, 1944.

[6] Sigmund Freud, *The Question of Lay Analysis*, with the author's 1927 Postscript, James Strachey Translation, p. 104. For a recent and brilliant reassessment of Freud, see Adam Phillips, *Becoming Freud: The Making of a Psychoanalyst*, New Haven, Yale University Press, 2014.

[7] *Ibid.*

[8] *Ibid*, p. 105

[9] *Ibid*, p. 99

[10] *Ibid.*

[11] *Ibid*, p. 108

[12] *Ibid*, p. 109

[13] Anton T. Boisen, "The Minister as Counselor," pp. 97-107, in Glen H. Asquith, Jr., *op.cit.*

Index

alcoholism, 87
Allen, Gene, 132
American Foundation of Religion and Psychiatry, 64
American Psychiatry Association, 129
American Psychosomatic Society, 20
Anton Boisen, 18, 78, 95, 96, 112, 115, 132, 140, 163, 176, 182
Association for Clinical Pastoral Southern Baptist, xx
Association for Clinical Pastoral Education (ACPE), xiii, xiv, xv, xviii, xx, xxi, 56, 57, 62, 64, 65, 66, 67, 68, 70, 71, 73, 75, 76, 78, 80, 82, 83, 85, 86, 87, 88, 90, 91, 92, 93, 94, 95, 96, 97, 98, 99, 100, 102, 103, 104, 105, 106, 109, 110, 111, 116, 119, 120, 121, 126, 130, 131, 132, 134, 135, 136, 137, 138, 139, 140, 141, 142, 147, 148, 149, 150, 151, 152, 165, 185, 209
Association of Mental Health Chaplains (AMHC), 17
Association of Pastoral Chaplains (APC), 134, 165, 166
Association of Theological Schools, 23, 55

Austin State Psychiatric Hospital, 85, 87

Barth, Karl, xix, 61, 123, 140, 142, 161, 166, 187, 191
Batchelder, Alice, 7, 14, 21, 23
Bean, Orson, 60
Bellow, Saul, 60
Benedict, Ruth, 29
Benson, Herbert, 169, 170
Bernays, Minna, 204
Bexley Hall, 10
Bickerton, Cathy, 119
Billinsky, John, 64, 65, 66
Bloom, Harold, 147, 148, 188
Bloomington, Indiana, 3
Bly, Robert, 136
Bogia, Ben, 132
Boisen, Anton Theophilus, iv, xiii, xiv, xv, xvi, xvii, xviii, xix, xxi, 1, 2, 3, 4, 5, 6, 7, 8, 9, 10, 11, 12, 13, 14, 15, 16, 17, 18, 20, 21, 22, 23, 25, 27, 28, 29, 31, 35, 36, 37, 40, 41, 42, 44, 45, 48, 49, 50, 51, 53, 54, 55, 56, 58, 59, 61, 65, 66, 67, 68, 73, 79, 81, 86, 95, 96, 112, 113, 114, 120, 121, 126, 132, 140, 141, 143, 145, 146, 151, 152, 153, 163, 170, 176, 177, 178, 179, 180, 181, 182, 183, 185, 186, 191
Boston Psychopathic Hospital, 7
Boswell, John, 129

Brigham, Tom, 47
Brinkman, Robert, 23, 27, 47, 51, 60, 62, 182
Browning, Don, 143
Bruner, Ernest, 47
Bruninga, Clarence, 16
Bryan, William, xvi, 9
Buck, George, 16, 62, 67, 85, 88, 114
Bunyan, John, 13
Byrd, Julian, 131, 140

Cabaniss, Don, 73, 152
Cabot, Richard, xiii, xix, xx, xxi, 9, 11, 12, 15, 16, 21, 22, 23, 25, 26, 35, 36, 37, 40, 41, 42, 44, 45, 46, 49, 51, 54, 58, 66, 67, 110, 126, 132, 140
Cadge, Wendy, 170
Cannon, Jr., James, 113
Capps, Donald, xxi, 143, 144, 145, 146, 171
Carlson, Walter, 112
Cedarleaf, Len, 66
Central State Hospital Milledgeville, 73, 208
Chicago Council for Clinical Pastoral Training, 12, 42
Chicago Theological Seminary, 11, 17, 23, 191
Childs, Brian E, viii, 30, 150, 204
Claytor, Robert, 91, 130
Coleman, Arthur, 94
College of Pastoral Supervision and Psychotherapy (CPSP), iii, xiv, xvii, xix, xx, 25, 58, 87, 91, 93, 94, 115, 116, 126, 130, 131, 132, 133, 134, 136, 138, 148, 149, 150, 153, 154, 185, 189, 190, 209
Columbia University, 19, 59
Committee of Twelve, 53, 54, 55, 97, 186
Connolly, Sean, 60
Contra Mundum, xvii, 98, 124, 154, 189, 209
Council for Clinical Training of Theology Students (CCTTS), xix, 1, 11, 21, 152

Dante, 18, 19, 164
Delosier, Zeke, 73
Deutsch, Helen, 19
Dialogue 88, xv, 116, 117, 119, 121, 122, 123
Dicks, Russell, 23, 35, 36, 37, 38, 39, 40, 41, 45, 46
Dictionary of Pastoral Care and Counseling, 125, 126, 128, 129
Dobson, Marcia Dunbar-Soule, 25
Duke University Hospital, 36, 37, 38
Dunbar, Helen Flanders, xvi, xx, 10, 11, 18, 19, 20, 21, 22, 23, 24, 25, 27, 28, 35, 42, 47, 51, 58, 59, 60, 61, 68, 120, 121, 132, 163, 177, 178, 181, 182, 183

Eastman, Fred, 8
Eckstein, Rudolf, 58
Eichorn, Herman, 16
Elgin State Hospital, 2, 4, 11, 12, 15, 16, 17, 23, 28, 151
Emmanuel Episcopal Church, 10
Emory University, 125

Falwell, Jerry, 127
Fletcher, Joseph, 28, 53, 55
Fortune, Marie, 154, 155, 160, 161
Fowler, James, 128
Fox, George, 13
French, Porter, 6, 27
Freud, Sigmund, xvi, xvii, xix, 2, 4, 6, 7, 8, 9, 13, 15, 19, 20, 22, 24, 25, 27, 28, 29, 33, 35, 37, 41, 42, 43, 44, 48, 49, 51, 56, 57, 58, 59, 61, 64, 65, 66, 67, 73, 112, 113, 127, 137, 143, 144, 145, 146, 147, 148, 151, 152, 168, 175, 176, 177, 178, 179, 180, 181, 182, 183, 191, 204
Freud's Trip to Orvieto The Great Doctor's Unresolved Confrontation with Antisemitism, Death, and Homoeroticism; His Passion for Paintings, 204
Fromm, Eric, 29
Fuller Theological Seminary, 125

Gable, Winton, 62, 63
Gay, Peter, 43, 44
Gilmore, John, 38
Ginsberg, Alan, 60
Goodman, Paul, 60
Guiles, Philip, 11, 35

Hall, Charles E., xx, 54, 64, 65, 66, 71, 73, 111, 112, 152
Hazelden Foundation, 86, 87
HealthCare Chaplaincy, 90
Helms, Jesse, 101
Hemenway, Joan E., 90, 165

Hiltner, Seward, xx, 6, 11, 16, 17, 23, 24, 27, 28, 29, 30, 31, 32, 33, 34, 49, 50, 51, 53, 58, 60, 61, 143, 166, 181, 191
Howe, Reuel, 47, 48
Hunter, Rodney J., 125

Indiana University, 3, 4
Institute for Pastoral Care, xix, 35

Jenkins, Jerry, 73
Jones, Alan, 128
Jorjorian, Armen D., xiv, 70, 71, 73, 74, 75, 77, 78
Journal of Pastoral Care, 28, 33, 65, 191, 209
Journal of Religion and Health, 93, 209
Jung, Carl, xvi, 13, 19, 42, 43, 44, 51, 54, 61, 64, 67, 127

Kean, Sam, 136
Keller, William S., 10
Kierkegaard, 147
Kinsey Reports
    Kinsey Institute, 30, 31, 32, 33
Klink, Tom, 16, 111
Knowles, Malcolm, 58, 66
Koenig, Harold, 168, 170
Kuether, Fred, 23, 47, 51, 52, 53, 56, 65, 111

Ladies Home Journal, 10
Lapsley, James, 128
Lebacqz, Karen, 137, 138, 139, 140
Lehman, Richard, 17, 47, 62
Lewin, S.A., 38

Lewis, Dean, 70
Lewisburg Federal Prison, 60

Madden, Ann, 148
Madden, Myron, xx, 49, 56, 57, 67, 73, 147, 150, 151, 152, 186
Mailer, Norman, 60, 161
Mansfield College, Oxford, 114, 208
May, Rollo, 29
Medical College of Virginia, 71
Mencken, H. L., 113
Meyer, Adolf, xvi
Miliyicertsova, Boshenyetu Gospondyna, 97
Miller, Perry, viii, 91, 130, 132, 205

National Council of Churches, 55
New England Theological Schools Committee on Clinical Training, 35, 45
New York Presbyterian Hospital, 8, 209
New York Psychoanalytic Institute, 20
New York Psychology Group, 29
Newhart, Bob, 62
Nichols, Edwin J., 100, 101, 102, 103
Nixon, Richard, 64
Nouwen, Henri, 4, 15

O'Connor, Sandra Day, 174
Oates, Wayne, xv, xx, 1, 2, 12, 17, 49, 55, 56, 57, 58, 67, 73, 147, 150, 151, 152, 153, 171, 185, 186
Olson, Cynthia, viii

orgone box, 24, 46, 60, 62

Palmer, Parker, 96
Parker, Duane, 96, 121
Patton, John, 73, 125
Peale, Norman Vincent, 64
Pendley, Howard, viii
Phoebe Needles Conference Center, 130
Playboy Mansion, 82
Poisoning of Eros, The, xv, 143, 153, 185, 186, 187, 209
Powell, Robert Charles, iv, xx, 95, 96, 132
Presbyterian Theological Seminary, 32, 70, 208
Prest, Pat, 71
Princeton Theological Seminary, xv, 27, 29, 32, 125, 143
Pruyser, Paul, 8, 16, 17
Puchalski, Christina, 168

Racial Ethnic Minority Conference, 102
Randolph-Macon College, 31
Reformation, 127
Reich, Wilhelm, 24, 27, 28, 46, 47, 48, 49, 51, 52, 54, 59, 60, 61, 62, 63, 67, 177, 178
Rentz, Medicus, 82
Rice, Otis, 47
Rimmer, Robert, 128
Rioch, Margaret, 94
Risted, Nick, 66
Roberts, David, 29
Rogers, Carl, 29
Rollman, John, 75
Roth, David, viii, 191
Roudinesco, Elizabeth, 4, 43, 44, 191

Rousseau, Jean-Jacques, 4
Ruether, Rosemary Radford, 136
Russell, Bill, 130

Salinger, J.D., 60
Schuller, Robert, 64
Schwartzenberger, Eugene, 116, 118
Sexual Revolution, xxi, 30, 31, 33, 37, 68, 75, 76, 80, 103, 114, 115, 128, 151, 172, 178
Shakespeare, William, 147, 150
Shepherd-Pratt Hospital, 11
Sherve, Al, 62
Southern Baptist Convention, 49
Southern Baptist Theological Seminary, xix, 2, 147, 188
Spickler, Emily, 52
St. Luke's Episcopal Hospital, 70, 71, 73
Stokes, Allison, iv, xx, 18
Stone, W. Clement, 64, 65
Sullivan, Chaplain Charles, 4, 15, 16
Sullivan, Harry Stack, xvi
Swedenborg, Emmanuel, 13
Swift, John, 92

Tavistock, 92, 93
Teer, John, 132
Thornton, Edward, xix, xx, 25, 49, 51, 52, 57, 62, 128, 191
Tillich, Paul, 29, 37, 61, 165, 166, 187
Tingue, Arthur, 64
Tolson, George, 66

Topeka State Hospital, 71
Towley, Carl K., 110
Turner, Cathy, 140
Turner, Phil, 139, 154

Underground Report, xvii, 91, 96, 98, 106, 116, 119, 120, 130, 155, 157, 160, 209
Union Theological Seminary, 6, 19, 20
University of Arkansas Medical Center, 87
University of Indiana, 31
University of St. Andrews, 114, 208

Vayhinger, John M., 128, 129

Wallace, H. Mac, 72
Weber, Nicholas Fox, 204
Westboro State Hospital, 4, 7, 8, 13
Wickes, Frances, 29
Wilkins, Ron, 73
Wilson, Chappell, 73, 132, 148, 152, 172, 174, 186
Wise, Carroll, 11, 17, 20, 23, 28, 35, 42
Wolf, Theodore, 23, 24, 47, 59, 60
Women Supervising Women, 83
Worcester, Elwood, xvi, 9, 10, 17, 20, 23, 28, 35, 48
Wynn, J.C., 128

Yale University, 19, 125, 147, 154
Young, Richard, 12, 152

POSTSCRIPT

APROPO OF FREUD'S OWN SEXUAL LIFE

After this monograph was declared finished and sent to the press, I was referred by Brian Childs to the just-published work of Nicholas Fox Weber, *Freud's Trip to Orvieto: The Great Doctor's Unresolved Confrontation with Antisemitism, Death, and Homoeroticism; His Passion for Paintings; and the Writer in His Footsteps,* (2017). It is an utterly marvelous, mesmerizing work, a hybrid of memoir and serious study of the life and person of Freud. Reading it I could hardly stop for meals. In the last pages of that book Weber points out that Sophie de Closets, his editor at the French publishing house, Fayard, gave him a book of Freud's travel letters. It seems that in 2007 a German researcher discovered that on August 11, 1898, the forty-two-year-old Freud and the thirty-three-year-old Minna Bernays registered as man and wife, under a pseudonym, at the Schweizerhaus, an inn in Maloja—a village high in the Swiss Alps, near St. Moritz. They stayed in room 11, one of the largest in the inn, for three nights. This hard data should put paid on any question of the relationship between Freud and Minna.

But Weber adds that we cannot be sure that the vacationing pair was having sex. He quotes his grandmother saying that you cannot be sure unless you're under the bed, and even then you can't be certain. True enough.

Then Weber goes on to point out that Freud wrote from that very hotel room loving letters to Martha, one beginning with "My dear treasure." Minna herself added three paragraphs of her own to this letter, beginning with "My dearheart..." and relating the marvelous sights, wonders of the glacier, the mountains and the lakes.

What do we make of this? Weber assesses these loving letters as evidence that there was likely no sexual relationship between Freud and Minna. "If a man was cheating on his wife, would he write such [letters to his wife]...?" asks Weber. To quote my psychotherapist friend Perry Miller, "If I had checked into a hotel room with a woman even more attractive than my wife, the first (or second) thing I would do would be to write a loving letter to my wife." Of course, Perry is a Christian, or at very least a product of Christianity and burdened as are all Christians with a bad conscience over sexual pleasure of any sort. If Freud and Minna indeed had a sexual relationship, would they have been burdened with guilt? I doubt it.

Freud's memory loss over the Orvieto's painter's name—his parapraxis—may well have stemmed from his cold fear of what exposure of his polygamy might mean in the anti-Semitic sex-phobic Austrian Catholic culture. Such fear would have been based in reality.

The point here is that Weber and virtually everyone who has commented on the likely bigamous relationship Freud had with Martha and Minna, simply fails to understand polygamous Judaism. The Talmud has guidelines about how a man should parcel out his sexual favors to his several wives so as to be a *just* husband. Freud was not an observant Jew, but he was a child of Judaism and influenced at least in part by Sephardic as well as Ashkenazi Judaism. Sephardic Jews have always tolerated polygamy. Ashkenazi Jews of the West adopted monogamy in medieval Europe under intense pressure from the Catholic authorities. But they assented with their fingers crossed, as preferable to being burned at the stake. And the Christian doctrine of perpetual monogamy was and is still alien to Jews and their religious literature, and in fact alien to the Judeo-Christian Bible itself.

Will we ever recover from the Christian loathing of sexual pleasure? Until we do, we will not be able to understand Judaism or Freud, or even, believe it or not, the Judeo-Christian Bible.

ABOUT THE AUTHOR

Raymond J. Lawrence is a Virginian by birth, which began his working life as a newspaper boy, then batboy for a professional baseball team, the Portsmouth Cubs. While in seminary he was ordained a Methodist minister and served rural churches in Chesterfield County, Virginia. Subsequently, he joined the Episcopal Church, was ordained priest, and served congregations in Newport News, Virginia, and Knoxville, Tennessee. He holds an M.Div. from Presbyterian Theological Seminary, in Richmond; an S.T.M. from the School of Theology, University of the South; and a D.Min. from New York Theological Seminary. He did two years of postgraduate studies at the University of St. Andrews in Scotland and at Mansfield College, Oxford University in England. He completed two years of clinical training in residencies at St. Luke's Episcopal-Texas Children's Hospital, in Houston, and at Central State Hospital, in Milledgeville.

His life's work has been principally in the field of clinical pastoral care and counseling and pastoral psychotherapy. He was certified clinical supervisor by the Association for Clinical Pastoral Education, in 1970, and held leadership positions with that organization. In 1988, he began publishing the ACPE *Underground Report,* which later morphed into *Contra Mundum.* In 1990, with colleagues, he founded the College of Pastoral Supervision and Psychotherapy and has functioned as General Secretary since. His last position was for 15 years as Director of Pastoral Care, New York Presbyterian Hospital, Columbia-Presbyterian Medical Center in New York City.

Lawrence has published widely in the fields of social ethics, sexuality, and religion. His articles have appeared in *The Journal of the American Medical Association (JAMA),* the *Annals of Behavioral Medicine,* the *Journal of Religion and Health,* the *Journal of Pastoral Care and Counseling, The Christian Century,* and others. His opinions have appeared in *The New York Times, The Washington Post,* the *Los Angeles Times,* and a number of other newspapers. He has written three books: *The Poisoning of Eros: Sexual Values in Conflict,* (Augustine Moore Press, 1989), *Sexual Liberation: The Scandal of Christendom* (Praeger Press, 2007), and *Nine Clinical Cases: The Soul of Pastoral Care and Counseling* (2015). He is an amateur mycologist and founder of the Texas Mycological Society. He may be reached at lawrence@cpsp.org.

Photo credit: Perry Miller

- Boisen
    - Exploration of the Inner World: A Study of Mental Disorder & Religious Experience
    - Out of the Depths

- Freud
    - Introductory Lectures

Made in the USA
Middletown, DE
12 May 2018